AN ADIRONDACK SAMPLER II

Backpacking Trips

by Bruce Wadsworth

ADIRONDACK MOUNTAIN CLUB
Glens Falls, New York

Reprinted with revisions, 1986.

Library of Congress Cataloging in Publication Data

Wadsworth, Bruce.
  An Adirondack sampler II.

  Includes indexes.
  1. Backpacking—New York (State)—Adirondack Mountains—
Guide-books. 2. Snow camping—New York (State)—Adirondack Mountains
—Guide-books. 3. Adirondack Mountains (N.Y.)—Description and travel—
Guide-books.
  I. Adirondack Mountain Club. II. Title.
GV199.42.N652A349   917.47'53   81-8089
ISBN 0-935272-15-1   AACR2

Printed in the
UNITED STATES OF AMERICA

CONTENTS

Key to Map

1. Pharaoh Lake Wilderness Area
2. Lake George Wild Forest Area
3. Siamese Ponds Wilderness Area
4. Wilcox Lake Wild Forest Area
5. West Canada Lakes Wilderness Area
6. Black River Wild Forest
7. Ha-De-Ron-Dah Wilderness Area
8. Pigeon Lake Wilderness Area
9. Santanoni Preserve
10. High Peaks Wilderness Area
11. Five Ponds Wilderness Area
12. Nehasane

iv

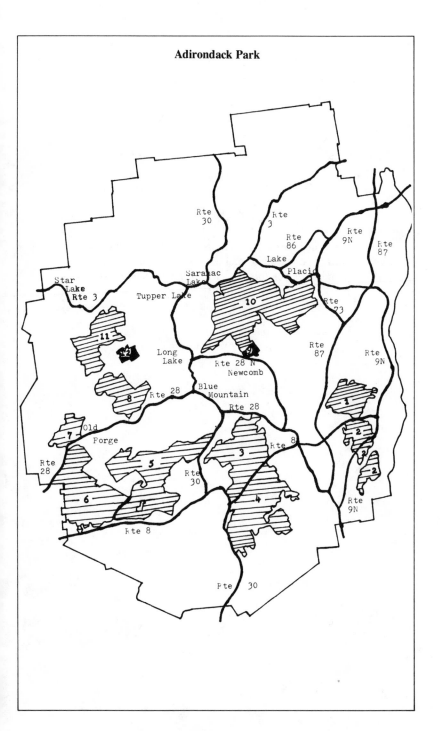

Adirondack Park

DEDICATION

This book is dedicated to those visionaries of yesteryear whose efforts saw the creation of the Forest Preserve. Because of their wisdom and struggles this magnificent public land exists today for all to use and enjoy.

Introduction

An Adirondack Sampler II, Backpacking Trips, is a sequel to *An Adirondack Sampler, Day Hikes for All Seasons.* Like the first volume, this book is for all seasons and covers a cross-section of the Adirondacks. Even many experienced Adirondack hikers are not familiar with that ninety percent of the Adirondack Park that is outside the High Peak Region; *An Adirondack Sampler II* describes a variety of backpacking trips throughout the Park for the novice and expert alike.

The trail descriptions are primarily two-day outings to accommodate weekend backpackers. In most cases, however, trips can be linked, or suggested options are given, so that the outings can be extended. These same factors will permit the fast-moving hiker to add items to his or her agenda. References to regional guides are given so that the reader can expand his experiences in the areas that might be particularly suited to his tastes and/or be close to home.

There are guidebooks for mountain climbers who backpack in order to reach the mountains, and there are guidebooks for backpackers who occasionally climb mountains because they happen to be on the trail being hiked. This book is the latter type. Except for the High Peaks section, the trips described here are not difficult with respect to terrain.

It is the author's belief that a sense of freedom and change from everyday routine are best achieved when time is spent enjoying the country one is passing through rather than on the physical challenge required to reach a destination. The backpacker should commune with, not try to conquer, nature. There should always be time enough to gaze at the scenery, and to think through one's thoughts. This book is for all who seek the camaraderie that comes from a shared wilderness experience, the glow of a campfire, and the sounds of darkness.

The reader should modify the outings described here to match his or her own goals, physical condition, and the experience of each individual member of the backpacking party.

Winter Camping

Many of the trips in this guidebook are highly suited to snowshoeing and ski camping. It is emphasized that inexperienced winter campers should take trips with those trained in winter survival techniques before setting out on their own in winter. The Adirondack Mountain Club chapters and many other organized groups provide this training. Winter conditions in the Adirondacks can be as severe as any place in the world. Do not take chances.

One of the best references for winter camping is *Winter Hiking and Camping* by John A. Danielsen, published by the Adirondack Mountain Club.

1

Corrections

Inevitably, trails change, beavers flood routes, and other factors occur which render a guidebook inaccurate. The user of this book is encouraged to report any errors or to suggest changes for future editions. Please send corrections and suggestions to the Adirondack Mountain Club, Inc., 174 Glen Street, Glens Falls, New York 12801.

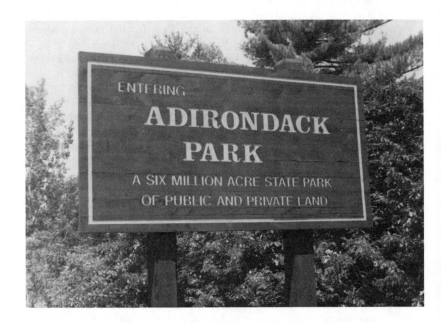

How to Use This Book

Certain methods, expressions, and techniques have been used in this book to convey precise information. This section should be read so that you will understand what these are and why they are used. This will permit you to use the book with greater facility and accuracy.

Trip Headings

DIFFICULTY. Difficulty generally refers to physical problems caused by terrain characteristics. Thus, a long flat hike is not considered difficult, even though it may be tiring. The good day hiker who zips along these trails will feel most of these hikes are easy. However, the overnight backpacker with thirty or forty pounds of gear on his back may consider the same trips much more difficult.

ROUND TRIP DISTANCE. Novices sometimes get in over their heads because they think only in terms of how far it is to a given destination, forgetting that an equal distance must be traveled on the return trip. Saying it is five miles to a given destination conveys something rather different than saying it is a ten mile round trip hike. Because loop trips often have different return distances from the outgoing section, it is often misleading to simply assume doubling the one way distance will be accurate.

TIME NECESSARY. The time given is that which most people seeking a relaxing trip will take. A day hiker could complete many of these trips in a single day, but the backpacker may choose to stay three days at a lake two miles from the trailhead before completing the trip. These are factors you must work out for yourself.

MAPS. Topographic maps are usually called quadrangles. Two long term changes are now occuring with maps which can cause confusion and which require careful attention when you are selecting maps. The first change concerns the *series* available and the second change involves the *units of measurement* used.

Series. In mapping, the term *minute* is used to represent an angle of measurement. There are 60 minutes in 1 degree. There are 360 degrees in the circle encompassing the earth. Thus, a 15-minute map shows the ground area which represents 15 minutes of longitude × 15 minutes of latitude. In the Adirondacks, a 15-minute map represents a ground distance of about 12.5 mi. (20 km) in an east-west direction and about 17.5 mi. (28 km) in a north-south direction.

A 7.5-minute map quadrangle represents only one-fourth the total map ground area and only one-half the ground distance in each direction as found on a

15-minute map. They permit greater detail since less ground area is represented on the same size sheet of paper as is used for a 15-minute quadrangle.

The abbreviation for minute is ', as in 15' map. Today certain 15' series map quadrangles have been replaced by four 7.5' map quadrangles. The information needed for the Five Ponds outing described in this guide, for example, can be obtained either from the 15' minute Cranberry Lake Quadrangle or from the Five Ponds 7.5' Series Quadrangle. The confusing thing is that there is also a 7.5' Cranberry Lake Quadrangle that wouldn't help you at all for this particular trip. So before purchasing maps, be sure to examine them carefully to be sure they have the information you need.

Units. New maps made by the United States Geological Survey (USGS) have metric units instead of the English units found on most maps today. The USGS is remapping the Adirondack Park, which will be the first area in the United States to be mapped in metric units. The Lake Placid and Saranac Lake Quadrangles were completed in metric units just prior to the 1980 Winter Olympics held in Lake Placid. These metric maps represent 15' longitude and 7.5' latitude. Their contour interval is 10 meters, which is larger than the 20 ft. contours the English unit maps currently use.

To help you through this transitional stage, both English and Metric measuring units have been used in this book, enabling you to use maps of either type. Compare the units, so that you gradually will become accustomed to the metric system.

STANDARD ABBREVIATIONS.

mi. = mile
yd(s) = yard(s)
ft. = foot, feet
in. = inch(es)

km = kilometer(s)
m = meter(s)
cm = centimeter(s)

39.4 inches = 1 meter
1000 meters = 1 kilometer
1 kilometer = 0.6 miles
1 mile = 1.62 kilometers

Directional Guidelines

1. As is standard practice, the right and left sides of a stream are determined as the observer faces downstream. Thus, if you are walking upstream on the right side of a southward flowing stream, you would be on the west bank of the stream.
2. Since you will be referring directly to your compass while hiking, compass readings have been given in the text.

If you take map angles to determine direction and intend to use a compass from those map angles, you must account for magnetic declination, which is approximately 15 degrees west in the Adirondacks. Converting map angles to compass angles must be done accurately to prevent your becoming lost in the woods. If you do not possess this skill, get a good book and study up on compass use before heading for the trail.

Land Classification

The Adirondack Park is approximately the size of the state of Connecticut. This is larger than the combined sizes of Yellowstone, Yosemite, and Glacier National Parks. Yet, if you asked a hiker where he went for the weekend, he is likely simply to say, "to the Adirondacks."

To encourage a better understanding of the Adirondack Park, the names of different areas as stated in the *Adirondack Park State Land Master Plan* have been used in this book.

The great majority of the publicly owned part of the Adirondack Park, ie. the Forest Preserve, is divided into one of three land classifications: Wilderness, Wild Forest, and Primitive Areas. Parts of the definitions of these three land classifications as found in the *Adirondack Park State Land Master Plan* follow.

The most wild and natural part of the Forest Preserve is the Wilderness Area: "Wilderness area, in contrast with those areas where man and his own works dominate the landscape, is an area where the earth and its community of life are untrammeled by man . . . where man himself is a visitor who does not remain." Wilderness Areas are usually 10,000 acres or larger in size. There are currently fifteen Wilderness Areas in the Adirondack Park.

In contrast, "A Wild Forest Area is an area where the resources permit a somewhat higher degree of human use than in Wilderness, Primitive, or Canoe Areas, while retaining an essentially wild character." One major difference between the two areas is that motorized vehicles are not permitted in Wilderness Areas, whereas they are permitted into Wild Forests under certain conditions. There are fifteen Wild Forest Areas in the Adirondack Park.

Primitive Areas are lands whose characteristics fall somewhere between those of the Wilderness and Wild Forest Areas. A truly wild land area may be classified as primitive if it is small and so affected by private land around it that it can never develop a wilderness character. Most Primitive Areas, however, are in a state of transition. Human use prior to becoming part of the Forest Preserve resulted in loss of wilderness characteristics. These characteristics will return in time and it is anticipated that these areas will eventually be reclassified as Wilderness Areas. There are nineteen Primitive Areas in the Adirondack Park.

Changes in Grade

The following drawings indicate how the terms *gradual, moderate, moderately steep, steep,* and *very steep* are used in this book.

GRADUAL

MODERATE

MODERATELY STEEP

30

STEEP

45

VERY STEEP

60+

Steepness Standards

6

Glossary

Bushwhack

To make one's way through bushes or undergrowth.

Cairn

A pile of rocks or stones to mark a summit or route.

Campsites

a) *Informal:* A campsite without structures, other than a fire ring. It may or may not conform to DEC regulations or the State Land Master Plan of the region.

b) *Designated:* A campsite marked with a sign (a teepee symbol) indicating a legal campsite in an otherwise nonconforming location.

c) *No Camping:* An old campsite no longer legally usable due to its nonconforming location. Marked with a sign (a teepee with an X through it).

Col

A pass across a ridge between two adjacent peaks.

Contour

An imaginary plane of unchanging elevation.

Corduroy

A road, trail, or bridge formed by logs laid side by side transversely to facilitate crossing swampy places.

Duff

Partly decayed vegetable matter on a forest floor.

Fork

A place where one road divides into two roads.

Hardwoods

Broad-leaf deciduous trees.

Lean-to

An open camp with overhanging roof on the open side.

Logging Road

A road used for removing logs from the forest. Many present-day hiking trails are on former logging roads.

Massif

A large rocky prominence.

Mixed Wood

A forest composed of both broad-leaf deciduous trees and cone-bearing coniferous trees.

Outcrop

A place where the bedrock of an area breaks the surface of the ground.

Paint Blazes

A blaze is where the bark of the tree has been cut to leave a scar. The scar is then painted to make an easily seen trail marker.

Softwoods

Cone-bearing coniferous trees.

Stillwater

A section of river where either natural or manmade barriers back up the water a long distance. Free flow of the stream is thus prevented.

Switchback

A sharp turn in the trail, made so that a generally desired direction can be maintained and at the same time the rate of incline of the trail can be kept moderate. Switchbacks occur in series on steep sections of trail.

Terrain

The surrounding land surface.

Topography

The degree of variation found in the terrain's elevation.

Vlei (vly)

An old Dutch term for a marshy or swampy area.

Cairn on Treadway Mountain

Trail Habits and Practices

The Adirondack Park consists of privately owned lands interspersed with the publicly owned Forest Preserve. Often the access trails to state owned land cross private property. They are kept open due to the courtesy and thoughtfulness of the landowners. It is important that the users of these private lands show the same courtesy and thoughtfulness by their actions and conduct.

The Forest Preserve is for all to use and enjoy. Sound forest practices will help sustain and improve the quality of both the land and the experience enjoyed by the backpacker.

Good trail manners make good friends. Good camping practices preserve the forest so that the next user will be able to enjoy it to its fullest extent. In addition, there are DEC regulations which must be followed. Some of the most basic of these manners, practices, and regulations are presented on the following pages. Woodswise campers know them to be sound. Beginners should adopt them.

Each user should consider himself a custodian of the land for future generations. It is not enough to love nature; it is necessary to carry out actions which will sustain and improve this great land.

ON THE TRAIL

1. For safety, hike in groups of four or more. Keep the group together. In case of injury, send more than one person for help to be sure the word gets through.
2. Be sure someone at home knows where you are hiking and your intended return time. Always sign in and out at trail registers.
3. Watch for trail markers. Know the general lay of the land you are traveling. Have both map and compass and know how to use them.

SELECTING CAMPSITES

1. Camping, except at designated sites, is not permitted within 150 ft. of roads, trails, springs, streams, ponds, and other bodies of water (DEC reg.).
2. Camp on high ground and away from water to find a favorable breeze and avoid bugs.
3. Lean-tos cannot be reserved. They are available to all campers on a first-come basis until capacity of the lean-to has been reached (DEC reg.).
4. It is wise to select a suitable camp early enough to get set up before dark. Keep a weather eye out to avoid having to make camp in the rain.

IN CAMP

1. Fires can be built only for cooking, warmth, or smudge (DEC reg.). Be careful if using tobacco.

2. It is illegal to cut live wood on state lands (NYS law). Cut only dead and down wood.
3. Use established privies whenever possible. If such privies are not available, make a slit trench well away from camp and from water. Be sure to cover human waste with soil and leaves. Burn toilet paper in winter.
4. Do not wash yourself, clothes, or dishes in a natural body of water. Use a container to collect water and use it away from the source. Use only biodegradable soaps and detergents. Dispose of waste well away from the source of water. Get drinking water upstream from your campsite.
5. You'll be more comfortable and have less difficulty with pests and animals if you keep food away from sleeping areas.
6. Hang food well away from the camping area, at least 15 feet up in the air and well extended from the reach of tree climbing bears. Do not leave snacks in your pack unless you want chipmunks and squirrels in your packs.
7. Set up tents in level or slightly rounded areas. Avoid low spots where rainwater will collect. It is not considered good practice to ditch tents.
8. Do not litter. Burn all burnables and remember that aluminum packages will not burn. Carry out all nonburnables.
9. Leave your campsite cleaner than you found it. It is an old custom to leave dry firewood for the next camper.
10. Do not leave boots or other items out where porcupines can carry them off.
11. No group of ten or more campers can camp on State Lands *at any time* except under permit (DEC reg.). Permits are available from the forest ranger in whose area you are camping.
12. Temporary camping in one location for more than three nights is prohibited except under permit (DEC reg.).
13. Use suitable filter or water purifier to insure against Giardia — especially in heavily used areas.

ON THE WAY OUT

1. If you carried it in full, you can certainly carry it out empty. Do not litter the forests. A good woodsman will leave his campsite in better condition than he found it. Take a litter bag along in your pack.
2. Mark OUT beside your name on the trail register, so others know you have returned.
3. Share your knowledge of problem areas or campsites with others you meet on the trail.

IF LOST

1. Sit down in one place for at least fifteen minutes to collect your senses. A simple overlooked fact that can unravel the problem will often come to mind.
2. If you are convinced you are really lost, find an open spot where aircraft can spot you. A nearby high land area may provide sightings that can be matched with your map to provide needed information. Do not wander aimlessly.
3. Pick a good place to stay. You will be found if you have let someone at home know where you are going and have given instructions for what to do if you are not home by a given time.

The Adirondack Mountain Club has several pamphlets of interest to the backpacker, *For the Day Hiker, For the Summer Backpacker, For the Winter Mountaineer, Hypothermia, Wilderness Tips, Biting Trail Bugs, Bear Facts,* and *Frostbite.* These may be obtained at small charge by writing the Adirondack Mountain Club, Inc., 174 Glen Street, Glens Falls, New York 12801.

Equipment and Vittles

The specific equipment you carry and the kinds of food you consume depend on many factors. How long will you be on the trail? What will you be doing? Is your budget large or small? How strong are you? Are you in good physical condition? Do you wish to rough it or smooth it? How many times a year do you use your gear?

Before making a significant investment, do some serious thinking about your real needs. Generally, five factors should be considered: comfort, adaptability to changing conditions, health, safety, and your personal interests. Rate any intended purchase against these five criteria. Serviceability will soon take precedence over such things as fancy laces, pretty decals, or color. Buy the best you can afford, but remember that no matter what the quality, you'll never enjoy using the equipment if it doesn't fit you well or if you don't feel comfortable with it.

Assimilate all the information you can from any and all sources, but base the final decisions upon your own assessment of how well the items meet the parameters you yourself have established.

An Adirondack Lean-to (Woodhull Lake)

Equipment

Following is a general listing of gear and things to consider when choosing equipment.

SUGGESTED PERSONAL EQUIPMENT

Sleeping bag and waterproof
   stuffbag
Rain protection (personal & pack)
Ground cloth
Foam pad (optional)
Water bottle/canteen
50 ft. of ⅛" nylon rope
Flashlight
Maps and compass
Tent with waterproof fly
Suitable pack
Insect repellent
Guidebook
Daily log book
Mosquito head net (in season)
Hat
Swim suit

Ditty bags for personal items
Camera (optional)
Fishing gear (optional)
Good hiking boots
Small/medium-sized knife
Plastic bags, assorted sizes
Books, playing cards (optional)
Gloves
Socks, extra sets
Jacket or sweater
Moccasins or sneakers
Long-sleeved shirt
Long trousers
Short pants (optional)
Handkerchiefs
Extra underwear

Repair kit:
   Sewing kit, safety pins, wire,
   pencil, paper, tent and pack
   repair kit, small pliers
Whistle
Matches

Toilet articles:
   Washcloth and towel, toothbrush,
   tooth paste, comb, hair brush,
   cream or lotion, soap, toilet
   tissue, sanitary items, nail file
   and clippers, unbreakable mirror,
   scissors

SUGGESTED COMMON EQUIPMENT

Water purification tablets or water filters
Salt tablets
First-aid kit:
  Sterile gauze
  Adhesive tape
  Bacitracin or other antiseptic
    creme
  Percogesic pills
  Zinc ointment
  Liquid ammonia
  Bee sting allergy treatment
    chemicals
  1 oz. green soap
  Band aids
  First-aid book
  Aspirin
  Milk of magnesia tablets
  Moleskin patches
  Special medications as needed
    (diabetes, epilepsy, etc.)
  1–6" bandage
  Scissors
  2–3 sterile needles
  1 tweezers
  1 ace bandage
Waterproof tape
Small needle-nosed pliers
Cooking gear and utensils
Plates, cups, silverware
Can opener
Biodegradable soap and scrubber
Cook stove
Fuel and fuel container
Collapsible water bucket
Food in waterproof bags
Small shovel or trowel
Litter bag

THINGS TO CONSIDER ABOUT EQUIPMENT

Sleeping bags

1. Synthetic materials are often preferable in the damp eastern United States; down loses its heating properties when wet.
2. Liners prolong the life of your sleeping bag and keep it clean.
3. Double bags can be used year-round.

Packs

1. External frames or internal frames are needed for backpacking.
2. A hip pad greatly increases personal comfort.
3. A pack must be large enough for the job and must fit well.

Tent

1. A tent is a necessity. You can not rely on having an empty lean-to.
2. Weight is important, but so is the amount of room needed. Will your gear fit into the tent if it rains?

Boots

1. Boots are your single most important equipment.
2. Boots must fit properly; break them in before taking a long hike with pack.
3. Medium-weight boots are needed when a heavy pack is used. Avoid heavy-weight boots designed for climbing Anapurna unless you are climbing Anapurna.
4. Moccasins feel awfully good around camp after a long day on the trail. Having an alternate set of footwear also allows your boots to dry out at night.

Cooking Gear

1. Carry a camp stove. Frequently used campsites will not have adequate firewood.
2. Consider the type of stove needed. Some fuels don't light easily in frigid weather. Will you need to melt a lot of snow for water? How many people will you be cooking for?
3. Consider the nestling cook kits. They are more bulky, but greatly simplify both food preparation and the cleaning of dishes.

First-Aid Kit

1. Carry a good one and know how to use it.
2. Extended wilderness trips require extra supplies of band-aids and perhaps an inflatable splint. One good complete kit per party is more useful than several individual kits.

Flashlight

1. The first time a porcupine is chewing at your sleeping bag in the dark you'll know why you need one.
2. Purchase one good one or you'll be forever buying cheap ones.
3. You can't carry a candle to the privy in a rain storm.

Rain Gear

1. A poncho should be large enough to cover both you and your pack.
2. If you prefer a rain jacket and rain chaps to a poncho, have a separate cover for your pack. A large plastic garbage bag works just fine.

Finally, the equipment won't do you any good unless you take it with you. Make a list of the equipment you want to take, or simply refer to the list in this book. Then check off the items as you pack.

In Transit

Some thought should be given to carrying your equipment in your vehicle from home to trailhead. Be sure your fuel can is safe and doesn't leak. Be careful that the upright canteen in your pack doesn't leak when you lay the pack on its side in the car trunk. Don't store your camera film in a hot car trunk.

When you start hiking, put your wallet, car keys, important papers, etc. in a small ditty bag. Then put the ditty bag in your pack. It's more comfortable to hike with empty pockets, and you won't lose the items on the trail or through a crack in the lean-to floor.

Vittles

The food you consume on camping trips should be nourishing and somewhat higher than normal in energy. There is, however, a vast difference between what the backpacker out for the weekend and the backpacker on the Northville-Placid Trail for two weeks needs to consider.

First of all, consider the total weight of food you can carry. The long-trip hiker has perhaps twenty meals to tote along. Weight is a factor. Dehydrated food (expensive) and freeze-dried food (very expensive) may well be needed to reduce the bulk and weight. On the other hand, the weekend camper probably has three meals to lug along. Weight won't be all that important, and under these circumstances practically anything can be carried.

The pancake mix in the supermarket is the same as the pancake mix in the camping store, so don't pay fancy prices for camping food even though you are going out for a week or more. In fact, granola, cool drink mixes, spaghetti, noodles, rice, dried meat, and numerous other foods are readily available in most food stores at a fraction of the cost camping stores will charge.

The weekend camper should consider what utensils are needed. Freeze-dried foods may only require adding hot water to the packages they come in, and if what you really want is a lazy weekend in the sun, or if you want shrimp cocktails, hollandaise sauce, and beef stroganoff without any mess or fuss, it may be worth your while to spend the extra money on camp food.

The point is that specially prepared camping food is a luxury, not a necessity, for backpacking.

The backpacker who uses nothing but dehydrated or freeze-dried food for extensive lengths of time may have another type of problem. The food is so concentrated and its roughage so reduced that normal bodily activities are prevented and the camper becomes constipated. Thus, it is wise to have a certain amount of fresh food in your diet. Stewed prunes may not be your choice for breakfast fruit, but many campers on long trips wish they had some.

Some backpackers prefer to have solid breakfast and end-of-day meals but no large time-consuming mid-day meals. Instead, they pack cheese, gorp, candy, and cookies. Then, whenever a rest break is taken during the day, they nibble and munch. This prevents that overstuffed feeling while you're hiking and insures a steady supply of nutrients all day long.

One last thing. Many people don't realize that water is a nutrient. See how long you can go without it! Trip planning should include knowing what water sources are along your route of travel. If the available supply is in doubt, carry a full water bottle. Drink it freely when needed. It is more important to you than food, since you probably have a little fat to give you energy.

Cooking Breakfast Trout

Pharaoh Lake Wilderness Area

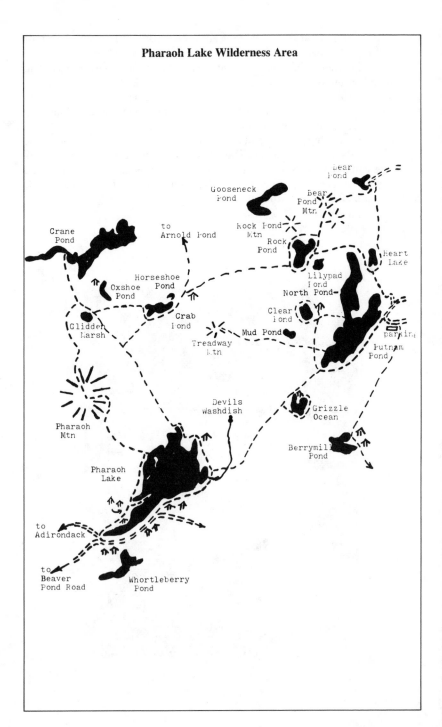

1. The Pharaoh Lake Wilderness Area

Pharaoh Lake Wilderness Area has perhaps the best network of foot trails in the Adirondack Park, outside of the High Peaks. Over 43,000 acres, plus the adjoining Crane Pond and Bald Ledge Primitive Areas, provide a combined total of 36.5 mi.(59.1 km) of foot trails.

There are thirty-five bodies of water in the Pharaoh Lake Wilderness Area and four more in the Crane Pond Primitive Area. Fifteen lean-tos are found in this region. Several of the ponds have been reclaimed and now have excellent trout fishing.

Pharaoh Mountain with its 2557 ft. (782 m) elevation is the highest peak in the region, but Owl Pate, Moose, Treadway, Putnam, and Knob mountains are all worth climbing. Many of the peaks and knobs of this section have bare rock summits which invite bushwhack trips into trailless areas. Though the mountain tops have relatively low elevations, the vertical ascent from base to summit is often considerable, since the base elevation of the whole region is also low. This is often overlooked by climbers who note only summit elevations and draw the erroneous conclusion that the only challenging climbs to be found are in the High Peaks.

The trips described here are reasonably short overnighters, but they can be linked to make a good week's outing. Actually, you could probably spend two or more weeks in this area and seldom retrace your steps. For instance, you might go from Rock Pond to Clear Pond to Grizzle Ocean, and then back to Putnam Pond to make a three day outing. On a week's trip you could extend on from Grizzle Ocean to Pharaoh Lake, over Pharaoh Mountain to Crane Pond, and then back to Rock Pond via Crab and Horseshoe Ponds. For more information about this region, see *Guide to Adirondack Trails: Eastern Region* by Betsy Tisdale (ADK).

Bear Pond–Rock Pond Loop and Options

Difficulty: Generally easy
Round Trip Distance: 6.0 mi.(9.7 km)
Time Necessary: 2 days
Map: Paradox Lake 15' Series

The trip goes from pond to pond in a leisurely fashion over excellent trails. It can easily be lengthened by visiting still more ponds or by bushwhacking a peak or two, and there are other possible trips if you really want to cover more ground. This outing is especially for the hiker who likes to study the fauna and flora, snap a few pictures, and maybe take a long afternoon swim. With full pack the trip will seem longer than it would appear to be on a map. Once in awhile it's nice just to take it easy and do a little fishing.

Trailhead access is from Putnam Pond Public Campsite and Day Use Area. It is reached off Rte. 74 from Ticonderoga in the east and from Exit 28 of the Adirondack Northway in the west. Turn off Rte. 74 at Chilson, where a large Putnam Pond Public Campsite sign is seen. It is 3.8 mi.(6.2 km) to the toll gate at the campsite. Bear right from the toll gate and, after crossing a bridge in a road dip, take the second lefthand turn. This takes you to the day use area, where your vehicle can be left in a large parking lot. Returning on foot to the road you turned from, turn left again and walk about 0.3 mi.(0.5 km). If you stay on the main road, you'll wind up around a grade and arrive at the trailhead, near Campsite #38. A signpost is located here.

DAY 1

The trail drops down a grade from the signpost (0.0 mi), curving northward beside the outlet of Heart Pond. Walking almost on the level, yellow DEC trail markers take you 0.3 mi.(0.5 km) to a junction within sight of Heart Pond.

The trail to the left leads to Rock Pond. Your route turns to the right, crossing the muddy outlet of Heart Pond on logs. The blue marked trail is noticeably less used than the trail on the earlier part of the hike. You swing past Heart Pond and continue northward through a splendid hardwood forest. Numerous white birches stand out in this section. The almost imperceptible grade and leaf covered trail make walking very enjoyable. Large hemlocks are occasionally seen, and at one point the trail crosses a base rock area. Here the woods open up and blueberries abound in season.

A T-junction appears at 1.4 mi.(2.4 km). The unmarked route to the right follows an old lumber road several miles to Chilson. Turn left and walk another 0.1 mi.(0.2 km). An unmarked path to the right leads over a knoll to the shore of Bear Pond. This pretty body of water has no obvious camp sites, but there are several spots that would be ideal.

Beyond the unmarked path, the trail reaches the southern end of Bear Pond in about 40 yds.(37 m). This part of the pond isn't nearly so attractive as that seen by taking the aforementioned path.

Turning abruptly left, the trail follows the edge of the pond, crosses its outlet on logs, and proceeds along the west shore. It then veers to the northwest and begins a long moderate climb up an old switchbacking tote road. At about 2.2 mi.(3.6 km), the 400 ft.(122 m) ascent brings you to a col having an approximate elevation of 1800 ft.(550 m).

An equally long grade takes you down to Rock Pond. The whole route from Bear Pond to Rock Pond is most interesting. At 2.9 mi.(4.7 km), the wide trail both narrows and steepens. Soon after crossing an open rock slide zone, you arrive at the shoreline of Rock Pond. A trail junction can be missed here if you are not careful. A red marked trail circles the pond to the right. The blue marked trail you have been following progresses to the left a short distance to still another junction.

(Several options are available to you at this point. Regardless of where you decide to go later, you should first visit the old iron mine which is a short distance along the red marked trail. Then, if you plan to camp on Rock Pond, you can continue along the red marked trail. If you wish a longer hike, you may choose to follow the blue marked trail to the next junction and head for Clear Pond or Lilypad Pond before setting up camp.)

The route suggested here swings to the right, following the red marked trail. Almost immediately a large iron cylinder is seen to the right; then old stone foundations whet your curiosity. Another 50 yds.(47 m) brings you to a fascinating old iron mine cutting into solid rock, and a side trail leads uphill past the mine a short way to the remains of a flooded open pit mine. These are two of the many abandoned mines which were operated during the Civil War and post-Civil War eras. The runoff carries a reddish iron material into Rock Pond, but it doesn't seem to affect its aquatic life, which is flourishing.

Beyond the mine, at 3.2 mi.(5.2 km), there are approximately 200 yds.(183 m) of somewhat hazardous trail. Here, a very steep rock wall requires you to sidle up a narrow trail; a hiker with full pack must be careful to maintain balance. It is not recommended if it is wet. However, the section is so short and what is beyond it so nice that there is every reason to continue along this route with suitable caution, in good weather.

Once past this point, the going is easier and you soon reach the great open rock formation that gives the pond its name. Rising out of the water, this massif makes an ideal place for a cooling swim and lunch break. In fact, there are several rough fireplaces found here. It would be an ideal camping spot. Between this point and the two lean-tos on the opposite side of the pond, you will find several more excellent campsites.

The pond trail circles to the north and becomes a very pleasant level route. It's a beautiful path, staying close to the water.

At 3.7 mi.(6.0 km) the Lilypad Pond trail comes in from the right. This trail leads 1.1 mi.(1.8 km) to Lilypad Pond, where a lean-to is located. From there, the trail branches left for Horseshoe Pond and right for Arnold Pond.

The pond trail continues on to the 3.9 mi.(6.3 km) point, where another junction is reached. Here, the Clear Pond trail enters from the right at an acute angle. It is 1.1 mi.(1.8 km) to Clear Pond, which has a lean-to on its eastern shoreline. Clear Pond has a trail around it, from which a trail to North Pond and another to Grizzle Ocean and Putnam Pond branch off.

The Rock Pond trail soon reaches the neck between Rock Pond and Little Rock Pond. This is crossed on a wooden bridge and brings you to another junction. The yellow marked trail to the right leads 0.1 mi.(0.2 km) to the Little Rock Pond lean-to. This lean-to is in excellent shape but is hidden in the trees, pointing away from the water. Why the almost perfect location for a shelter just before the lean-to was overlooked is hard to explain.

The pond trail now follows yellow markers north of this junction. At 4.2 mi.(6.8 km) the Rock Pond lean-to is reached. It sits surrounded by large trees back a short distance from the shoreline.

From here it is only 0.1 mi.(0.2 km) to another junction. A very short distance around the pond from this junction will bring you to the Bear Pond trail junction mentioned at about 3.0 mi.(4.9 km).

A right turn at this junction leads to North Pond.

DAY 2

It is assumed you camped somewhere around Rock Pond on Day 1. A long hike can return you to Putnam Pond Campsite via Clear Pond and the eastern shore of Putnam Pond.

The described route is a much shorter trip. Beginning at the junction previously mentioned at the 4.3 mi.(7.0 km) point, turn right and proceed towards North Pond. At 4.5 mi.(7.3 km), a junction is reached. Here, a yellow trail leads to Lilypad Pond (not the same one mentioned earlier) and then to Clear Pond.

Continue straight ahead for North Pond. A short moderate grade takes you over a ridge, and a longer moderate grade takes you down to junction within sight of North Pond at 5.0 mi.(8.1 km). North Pond was once distinct from Putnam Pond, connected by a narrow channel through a marshy area. Construction of the dam at the Putnam Pond outlet raised the water level. Modern maps make North Pond seem to be only a lobe of Putnam Pond.

A sharp left at this junction takes you through a series of short moderately steep ups and downs. At 5.6 mi.(9.1 km) an unmarked path to the left, just before a steep dip, guides you out to a high peninsula jutting out into Heart Pond. This beautiful little spot is a good place for a short photographic break.

The Bear Pond junction is reached at 5.7 mi.(9.2 km). It is only 0.3 mi.(0.5 km) straight ahead to the trail head at Putnam Pond Public Campsite.

Grizzle Ocean and Treadway Mountain

Difficulty: Easy trail, easy mountain.
Round Trip Distance: 7.4 mi.(12.0 km)
Time Necessary: 2 days
Map: Paradox Lake 15′ Series

This can be an extremely easy beginner's outing into Grizzle Ocean for a total 3.8 mi.(6.2 km) round trip if Treadway Mountain is skipped. However, Treadway Mountain should not be skipped. It is a remarkably easy mountain to climb, even with full pack. Offering a full circle vista from its bare, solid quartz summit, you'll spend a long time gazing out at the surrounding lakes, ponds, and forest before leaving it. The descent will get you over to Grizzle Ocean for a refreshing swim before supper. It's not very big, and there's no salt air breeze, but it's the only "ocean" we've got in the Adirondacks.

Access to the trailhead is from the toll booth at the Putnam Pond Public Campsite and Day Use Area. Refer to the Bear Pond– Rock Pond Loop trip and use the same directions for arriving at the campsite.

From the toll booth, take the left side of the fork in front of you. Drive along Putnam Creek to Putnam Pond. Continue past the boat launching site, at 0.2 mi.(0.3 km). Swinging around a bend to the left, the trailhead signs are soon seen. A large parking area is on the right, just beyond the trail signs. (Do not mistakenly take the Berrymill Pond trail, which begins at the far end of the parking area.)

The trail begins at the DEC trail signs (0.0 mi.) at the west end of the parking area. Follow yellow trail markers over minor ups and downs that will soon level out as you walk along the east shore of Putnam Pond. An unmarked trail forks right, five minutes down the trail. It leads 0.1 mi.(0.2 km) to a picnic table on the shore of Putnam Pond.

Bearing left from the fork, the route moves back from the pond. Before long, you begin a gradual upgrade. The way becomes quite rocky, developing a moderate grade through a splendid grove of hemlocks. Height of land is soon reached at 0.7 mi.(1.1 km), where a moderately steep descent continues through hemlocks.

A split log bridge takes you over the large outlet of Berrymill Pond. Five minutes later, a trail junction with signs is reached. This is the 1.2 mi.(1.9 km) point. Here the side trail leads 0.1 mi.(0.2 km) to the right to a boat landing.

Continuing straight ahead for another ten minutes brings you to another split log bridge. Crossing over the outlet of Grizzle Ocean, another trail junction is immediately seen, at 1.4 mi.(2.3 km). The yellow trail straight ahead leads 0.5 mi.(0.8 km) to Grizzle Ocean. The continuing trail description takes you up Treadway Mountain before heading for Grizzle Ocean from this junction. This stream is the last sure water on the summit trail.

Turn right and follow the blue marked Clear Pond trail towards Treadway Mountain. Rolling terrain is easily traveled as you skirt a small vlei. A four-way trail junction is reached at 1.8 mi.(2.9 km). The trail straight ahead continues another 0.4 mi.(0.6 km) to Clear Pond, which has a lean-to. The trail right leads 0.2 mi.(0.3 km) to a boat landing on Putnam Pond. Snowshoers ascend Treadway in winter by walking the Putnam Pond ice to this boat landing.

Turn left and follow red trail markers. A short moderate slope soon levels. Comfortable trail takes you around the south edge of a beaver bog near Mud Pond. A rocky outcrop is passed. The trail turns left after crossing a brook on a log bridge. Level trail becomes a gradual upgrade and then briefly a moderate grade before again leveling off. The mixed wood forest has some large beech and maple. No sustained difficulties present themselves to the hiker with a full pack.

You continue up varying grades with intervening level stretches where you can catch your breath. A bare rock slide zone is seen through the trees to the right. The trail threads its way into a narrow gorge, and the way becomes quite rocky for a short time. Then at 2.6 mi.(4.2 km) the trail is steep for 50 yds.(47 m) before bursting out onto open rock.

The rest of the ascent is a long, gradual to moderate grade over open rock with occasional dips into wooded gullies. White pines are dispersed on the slopes, and blueberries are everywhere. Large rock cairns guide you. Views begin to open up behind you to the east as you climb. Vermont's Green Mountains are profiled on the distant horizon, and glimpses of Lake Champlain can be had by careful observers.

A rim is reached at 3.0 mi.(4.9 km), where you gain your first sighting to the south and west. Magnificent Pharaoh Lake lies below you in the shadows of Pharaoh Mountain. The firetower on Pharaoh Mountain stands out in the west. Treadway's summit is before you, to your right front.

Some backpackers may not wish to proceed beyond this point, since there is a fairly steep col followed by a long, moderate climb to the peak's summit. However, with a few minutes rest the pack won't seem so heavy, and there's a

Pharaoh Lake

great view to the north from the summit. The High Peaks of Mount Marcy and her court stand out in full glory to the north.

The summit is reached at 3.2 mi.(5.2 km). Summit elevation is 2248 ft.(687 m) and ascent from the last trail junction is 848 ft.(259 m). The bulk of the mountain top is milky quartz; if you look carefully, some outstanding rose quartz can be found. A long leisurely lunch has been earned, and this summit is the perfect place to enjoy it.

When you can pull yourself away, return to the Grizzle Ocean outlet junction, which will be reached at 5.0 mi.(8.1 km). Turn right at the trail junction and follow yellow trail markers. Your course parallels the outlet stream, which you soon cross. The gradual upgrade takes you to a trail junction at 5.4 mi.(8.7 km). The trail straight ahead leads 2.5 mi.(4.1 km) to Pharaoh Lake via Wolf Pond.

Turn left from the junction and walk along a blue marked trail 0.1 mi.(0.2 km) to the lean-to at Grizzle Ocean. The lean-to, at 5.5 mi.(8.9 km), sits back from the shore, surrounded by well thinned trees. Across the "ocean" is Thunderbolt Mountain, an easy bushwhack. An informal path leads around the shoreline. Approximately 0.1 mi.(0.2 km) around the northwest shore is a very nice informal campsite.

The return trip to the parking area is 1.9 mi.(3.1 km). This makes a total round trip distance, including Treadway Mountain, of 7.4 mi.(12.0 km).

Pharaoh Mountain—Pharaoh Lake Loop

Difficulty: Moderate
Round Trip Distance: 13.4 mi.(21.7 km)
Time Necessary: 2 days
Map: Paradox Lake 15' Series

DAY 1

Beginners who haven't learned to pace themselves may feel this is a tough hike. But if you leave yourself plenty of time for the ascent of Pharaoh Mountain and rest when it's necessary, you'll find this is really not a rough trip at all. Once at the summit the rest of the trip is a breeze.

Pharaoh Lake is a large lake with several lean-tos along its shorelines. It has good fishing and is rather scenic, with rocky outcrops and tall white pines displaying considerable beauty.

Access to the trailhead is from Crane Pond. If approaching from the Adirondack Northway (Interstate 87), exit at Interchange 28. Follow Rte. 74 east a short distance to Rte. 9. Turn right (south) and drive 0.5 mi. (0.8 km) to a road junction. Turn left onto Alder Meadow Road. Bear left at a fork in this road 2.2 mi. (3.2 km) from Rte. 9. Travel another 1.4 mi. (2.2 km) to the winter parking area at the end of this road. In the summer you may turn right and follow Crane Pond Road another 1.9 mi. (3.0 km) to the DEC parking area at Crane Pond. Crane Pond Road is a narrow dirt road where low speeds and careful driving are required. In 1980 town road crews improved the road somewhat, so that it is relatively easier to travel than in prior years. Unfortunately, this improved condition tends to result in overuse of Crane Pond by weekend campers, especially on holiday weekends.

Sign in at the trail register (0.0 mi.). The fire tower on Pharaoh Mountain is 2.8 mi. (4.5 km) away. A 1257 ft. (384 m) ascent is required to reach the 2557 ft. (782 m) summit. Be sure to take plenty of water.

Cross the foot bridge over Crane Pond outlet and follow red DEC trail markers up an old logging road to the south. Soon you will be in the Pharaoh Lake Wilderness Area. The attractive mixed wood forest has easy ups and downs which are enjoyable.

A trail junction is reached at 0.7 mi. (1.1 km). The Pharaoh Mountain trail makes a sharp right and then a left across a bridge before straightening out again. The lower slopes of the mountain give no trouble, but the grade progressively steepens as you climb. Take shorter steps and rest your pack occasionally. You are encouraged to follow the hiking trail rather than the steeper telephone line.

In the upper third of the mountain, you will cross a rocky creek where the fire observer has put white markers on some of the trees. Though the stream may be dry in the summer, there is usually water coming from a large rock in the stream. This is the last water before the summit.

The trail now becomes very rocky. Views begin to open up to the west. Goose Pond may be visible behind you to the north. One last, steep incline brings you to the fire observer's cabin and the fire tower. In 1986 hikers were allowed up the fire tower but because of its condition this may be temporary. Excellent views are available without using the tower. Spectacle Pond, Desolate Brook, and other bodies of water are to the west. You may be fortunate enough to see turkey vultures gliding above the cliffs to your left front. By going a short distance southwest to another vantage point, a good view of Pharaoh Lake is obtained.

This summit makes a good snowshoe trip of 9.4 mi. (15.2 km) round trip from the winter parking area. Some people ski to the base of the mountain before donning snowshoes for the ascent.

The descent to Pharaoh Lake begins at a trail to the rear of the fire observer's cabin. It initially heads eastward before swinging to the south. The upper section is quite steep in places as the trail cuts between large boulders. These moss covered giants are most interesting. At approximately 3.3 mi. (5.3 km), a ledge provides good viewing. The trail now levels for awhile. The rocky route follows a ridge contour which offers fine vistas to the east.

At 3.7 mi. (6.0 km), the trail begins a moderate grade descent again which continues to the lake shore. A trail junction is reached about 50 ft. (15 m) from the lake. You'll probably continue on for this short distance to the boat landing to get a refreshing drink of water and take a well deserved rest by the shore. What appears to be the opposite side of the lake is actually a large island.

Climbing the short distance back up the trail, turn left (south). The red marked trail continues well above the water, generally following the contours of the land. Occasional minor knolls are crossed until you again find yourself near the shoreline of the lake at 5.3 mi. (8.6 km).

Here, a trail junction is found. To the left, a yellow marked trail leads back along a peninsula to two lean-tos, which are reached at 5.7 mi. (9.2 km). The first is 200 ft. (61 m) from the end of the peninsula. This is a double lean-to and can hold at least fifteen campers. The second lean-to sits out on the point of the peninsula a few meters above the water. The setting is magnificent. To sit on the tip of this peninsula in the early morning, watching the mist rise as ducks and loons swim around the lake, is an experience not soon forgotten.

DAY 2

Retrace the 0.4 mi. (0.6 km) to the trail junction. Continue southward along the red marked trail. The terrain becomes more rugged, but is still not difficult. At approximately 0.9 mi. (1.5 km) the attentive hiker will spot a lean-to along the shoreline, several meters through the trees. No side trail is immediately evident, so some care is needed or you will miss it. Again you veer away from the water and gain some elevation. Some bare rock outcrops are crossed before the trail drops down to the bridge over the outlet of Pharaoh Lake at 1.2 mi. (1.9 km).

Just before crossing the bridge, you'll notice a trail cutting back sharply to the right rear. It leads to a spring, which doesn't always flow clearly. Across the bridge is a grassy slope that looks like it has always been there. Actually, this little meadow is where an interior ranger's station stood for many years. It was removed in 1978 to make the region better conform to the legal definition of wilderness, wherein manmade permanent structures should not be found.

An old logging road bears to the right. Today, it is a foot trail and leads approximately 3.0 mi. (4.9 km) to Beaver Pond Road near Brant Lake. This is the closest direct route to Pharaoh Lake from a road.

The trail around the lake continues to the left, heading up a gradual slope, now following a yellow marked horse trail. After a short distance you reach a barn with stalls for horse backpacking trips. Nearby are two lean-tos, used primarily by horseback riders.

Proceeding along the logging road, a double-sized lean-to is found after a ten minute walk.

At 2.2 mi. (3.6 km) a junction is reached a short distance from this lean-to. The hiking trail forks to the left toward the lakeshore, whereas the horse trail continues to the right along the road to Springhill Ponds. Keep a sharp lookout for this turnoff. After crossing a small stream, a sidetrail leads to a lean-to near the lake. Informal campsites dot this section of the lakeshore.

The trail steepens at 2.8 mi. (4.5 km). You are soon high above the lake, sidling along a steep-sided ridge. As you descend again towards the water, a large beaver house can be seen in the bay. The trail levels a bit and is easier for walking.

A trail junction appears at 3.2 mi. (5.2 km). The trail coming in from the right leads 2.5 mi. (4.1 km) to Grizzle Ocean via Wolf Pond. Bearing to the left, continue northward towards Winter Green Point. At approximately 3.6 mi. (5.8 km) the route swings around the end of the bay and heads westward until the last lean-to on the lake is reached at 3.9 mi. (6.3 km). This is a nice lean-to and makes a good place for a lunch or rest stop.

The route from the lean-to leads northward around Split Rock Bay. This huge cleaved boulder stands like a sentinel in the narrow bay. A deliciously cool spring comes out of the slope on the right at 4.1 mi. (6.6 km). Here, at the tip of the bay, is a good place to fill up on water before beginning the steep climbing just ahead.

A few minutes after leaving the spring you start a moderately steep ascent up a grade for 0.2 mi. (0.3 km). Some conveniently placed boulders near the top of grade, 300 ft. (92 m) above the lake surface, make good seats to rest on.

The trail takes you to the northwest along the eastern base of Pharaoh Mountain. Nearly level for the first 0.5 mi. (0.8 km), it thereafter becomes a gradual downgrade and eases your travel for the remaining distance to Crane Pond. It is a very enjoyable stretch of trail, though past strong winds have caused frequent blowdown of aging beeches in several places.

A junction is reached at 6.0 mi. (9.7 km). The red marked trail to the right leads 0.5 mi. (0.8 km) to Crab Pond and 1.2 mi. (1.9 km) to Horseshoe Pond. From Horseshoe Pond it is possible to loop over to Oxshoe Pond. Beyond Horseshoe Pond one can hike much further to Arnold Pond or connect into the Putnam Pond area via Rock Pond.

Continuing straight ahead on the yellow marked trail, the inlet to Glidden Marsh is crossed on a bridge at 6.3 mi. (10.2 km). Soon Glidden Marsh is seen on the left. This is a beautiful body of water, teeming with wildlife. Numerous beaver dams are seen, and birdlife abounds. The open water is seen through magnificent white birches as you walk along an old woods road on the northeast side of the marsh.

The trail to Oxshoe Pond enters from the right at 6.7 mi. (10.9 km). Oxshoe Pond is 0.3 mi. (0.5 km); a lean-to is found on its southern shoreline.

The trail ahead narrows as it passes along the left side of a wet area. It then swings over a small rise and soon comes to the Pharaoh Mountain junction at 7.0 mi. (11.3 km).

Bear right and walk along the grassy road 0.7 mi. (1.1 km) to Crane Pond. The parking area is reached at 7.7 mi. (12.5 km).

2. The Lake George Wild Forest Area

The east side of Lake George is a little known section of the Adirondack Park. You don't find yourself there by accident; you have to head into this isolated country by design. Filled with historical interest, thirty miles or more of hiking trails make it a place worth heading for.

The Lake George– Lake Champlain Corridor is where much of both the French and Indian War and the Revolutionary War were bitterly fought. The flitting shadows of Roger's Rangers were all that were seen on cold winter nights as the scouts headed north on forays. And it was in the dead of winter that Henry Knox struggled down Lake George on ice transporting Fort Ticonderoga's cannon to siege Boston. It's not hard to imagine Mohawk warriors paddling a tortured Father Isaac Jogues to martyrdom at Ossernenon on the Mohawk River. The woods seem full of the spirits of Duncan Campbell, Colonel Munro, and the Marquis de Montcalm. To a student of American history it is hard to imagine a more fascinating activity than spending a day atop one of the lake's open mountain peaks, reliving the past.

In the midst of this Yorker heritage are over thirty lakes and ponds surrounded by hemlocks, pines, and birch. Beaver are found on every body of water. Ducks fly in and out continually. There are mountains to climb and the fishing is good.

The Lake George Wild Forest Area straddles the central portion of Lake George. Trails in the Tongue Mountain Range on the west side of the lake are not recommended for summer backpacking because there is no water to be found on the high trails that follow down the spine of the range. Much summer day hiking is done here, however, since the small amounts of water needed for a day hike can easily be carried. (Refer to *An Adirondack Sampler, Day Hikes for All Seasons,* ADK publication.) The Tongue Range does provide excellent snowshoe backpacking in the winter, when snow can be melted for water.

The part of this wild forest area on the east side of Lake George is quite different. Here an ideal environment and almost limitless trails provide rewarding outings.

There is an occasional report of rattlesnakes at Shelving Rock and on Black Mountain in the summer months but, while some care should be taken in these two areas, the hiker should not be unduly concerned. As a precaution, look at the far side of logs before stepping over them, and be careful where you place your hands when climbing steep rocky zones.

There are three access points to the hiking areas on the east side of Lake George: Pilot Knob, Shelving Rock Road, and Huletts Landing. All three are best reached from Interstate 87 by exiting at Interchange 20 at Lake George. Turn left onto Rte. 9, and then turn right toward Whitehall when you reach Rte. 149.

If you wish to go to Pilot Knob, proceed along Rte. 149 until you reach Rte. 9L, just past a golf course. Turn left onto Rte. 9L and travel northward until you

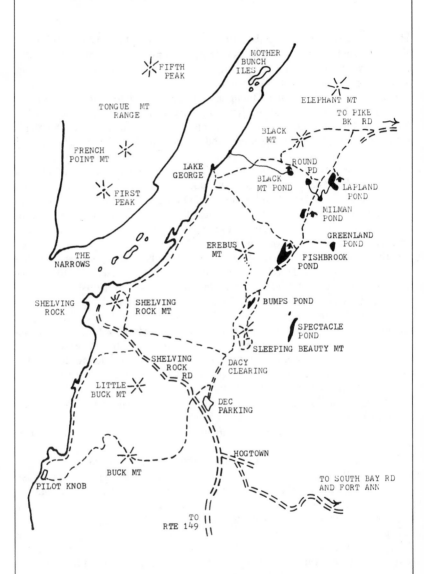

Lake George Wild Forest Area

come to a right hand turn for Pilot Knob and Katterkill Bay. This is Pilot Knob Road. Drive approximately 3.0 mi. (4.9 km) along Pilot Knob Road to the DEC parking lot and signpost on the right side of the road.

The DEC parking area on Shelving Rock Road is best reached by driving along Rte. 149 towards Whitehall. After Rte. 9L, continue on Rte. 149 for 1.5 mi. (2.4 km) until you reach Buttermilk Falls Road. This road is on the left; there is a store called The Black Rooster at the intersection. From here it is 9.8 mi. (15.9 km) to the Shelving Rock parking area. Buttermilk Falls is seen behind a home on the left at 1.4 mi. (2.3 km), and the road merges into Sly Pond Road at 4.1 mi. (6.6 km). The DEC Inman Pond trail up Buck Mountain is passed on the left at 6.5 mi. (10.5 km). Continue to the Hogtown Road intersection at 9.0 mi. (14.6 km). Continue straight ahead on the road you have been traveling for another 0.8 mi. (1.3 km) until you reach the DEC parking area, where a large sign reads "Lake George Horse Trails."

This parking area can also be reached from Fort Ann. In Fort Ann, turn off Rte. 4 onto County Road 16 (Charles St.) at the Portage Restaurant. This road leads towards South Bay through a most attractive rural valley. A large open gravel pit is passed at 5.9 mi. (9.6 km) from Fort Ann. Hogtown Road is reached 0.3 mi. (0.5 km) past this gravel pit. Make a left hand turn onto this road, which has no identifying sign. This is a very narrow unpaved road which can be in very poor condition during the spring mud season. The Buttermilk Falls Road described above is a much better route.

The Huletts Landing DEC parking area is reached by following Rte. 149 to Fort Ann. Turn left onto Rte. 4 and drive to Whitehall. Continue through Whitehall, where the road you have been traveling on becomes Rte. 22. Approximately 4.5 mi. (7.3 km) north of the point where Rte. 22 crosses Lake Champlain's South Bay you will reach the road for Huletts Landing. Turn left and proceed 2.7 mi. (4.4 km) to Pike Brook Road. Turn left again and travel another 0.8 mi. (1.3 km) on Pike Brook Road. As you begin to descend a hill, the parking area and a large DEC sign is seen on the right. This is 3.5 mi. (5.6 km) from Rte. 22.

This region offers a wide variety of backpacking opportunities. The length of time available, pace desired, and specific activities to be carried out will all affect your final selection of route. A map has been provided to help you make your decision.

Following are detailed trail descriptions of two rather lengthy trips into this country. While not everyone will have the time or inclination to do each of these in their entirety, most of the trail system in this area has been described. From them you will be able to put together outings tailored to your own needs and interests. For additional information, see *Guide to the Eastern Adirondacks* (ADK).

No unassigned overnight camping is permitted along the Lake George shoreline from Shelving Rock to Black Mountain Point. Arrangements to camp there must be made through the DEC in the same manner that one obtains camping spots on the state owned islands of Lake George.

Travel from the lakeshore inland is uphill and moderately steep. Black Mountain Pond, for instance, is approximately 1400 ft. (428 m) above Lake George.

North-south routes are relatively less strenuous than are east-west routes. The shoreline trails are best hiked in the spring time or in early fall before hunting season opens. At these times you will have the trails to yourself. At other times, hunters or boat campers may detract from your enjoyment, since differing activities are not always compatible.

Fishbrook Pond and Sleeping Beauty Mountain

Difficulty: Moderate
Round Trip Distance: 12.7 mi. (20.6 km)
Time Necessary: 2 days
Map: Bolton Landing 15′ Series

Fishbrook Pond and Sleeping Beauty Mountain make an ideal backpacking trip for a weekend outing. The trail head is at the DEC parking area on Shelving Rock Road. The route is generally along an old horse road with varied terrain. This would also make a good winter cross-country ski trip, though snowmobiles may be encountered. Be sure to sign the trail register. Trailhead elevation is 1208 ft. (369 m).

Always follow the small circular foot trail markers. Horse trail markers (with a horsehead on them) and snowmobile markers (about twice as large as the others) will also be seen. Since the horse and snowmobile trails often coincide with the foot trails, a watchful eye is needed to maintain the proper route.

DAY 1

The trail to Fishbrook Pond follows yellow trail markers from the barrier (0.0 mi.) at the rear of the parking area. The gravel road has minor ups and downs. At 0.5 mi. (0.8 km) a small DEC signpost is passed. Another 200 ft. (61 m) along the trail there is a junction where a yellow marked horse trail bears to the left. Avoid it.

Continuing along your route, Dacy Clearing is reached at 2.2 mi. (3.6 km). Just as you enter the clearing, another dirt road comes in from the left. It has yellow horse trail markers and heads to the east.

Dacy Clearing is an interesting place. Foundations of an old homestead are seen at various points around the clearing. A few tie-up railings for horses are also scattered here and there. Standing out starkly against the distant sky, the reclining profile of Sleeping Beauty Mountain presents an inviting vista to the north. From this great precipice, one has one of the finest views in the Lake George region.

Dacy Clearing is constricted in the middle and so really is almost two clearings. Your route crosses the first one before circling down a small grade to a stream. A bridge is found here and from it the road winds upward to the second clearing. It is evident that this site is sometimes used for camping, but only an emergency should make its use necessary. At the far end of the open area, somewhat hidden by the trees on the left side, a blue markered horse trail leads 3.1 mi. (5.0 km) to Shelving Rock Road.

Another barrier blocks the north end of the clearing. You have now traveled 2.5 mi. (4.1 km); this is a good place to take a break before beginning the next section. Beyond the barrier, a rock filled road angles up the side of the ridge in broad switchbacks towards Sleeping Beauty Mountain. Before the next junction is reached, 500 ft. (152 m) elevation will be gained.

The junction is reached at 3.4 mi. (5.5 km). The yellow marked trail turns abruptly to the right onto what appears to be a broad rolling trail. After about 0.2 mi. (0.3 km), however, this old bridal path begins a series of steep switchbacks that make for a rather rugged ascent if you are toting a full backpack. It is therefore recommended that you use instead the red marked trail straight past this junction and continue on to Bumps Pond. Sleeping Beauty Mountain should be climbed, but will be surmounted far more easily if climbed from the north by its other trail on the return trip.

Steady climbing commences immediately on the red marked trail, but at a moderate grade. Two excellent lookouts to the southwest are passed. Height of land is reached at 2160 ft. (661 m). You have gained 952 ft. (291 m) since leaving the parking area.

The trail drops in elevation and circles the west side of Bumps Pond, where a chimney is all that remains of a cabin. A junction (somewhat flooded due to beaver activity) is a short distance past the chimney, at 4.4 mi. (7.1 km).

A DEC sign states (erroneously) that it is 0.6 mi. (1.0 km) to Erebus Mountain. Actually, a yellow marked trail leads 0.3 mi. (0.5 km) to a fine view of Lake George at Bumps Pond Lookout, and from there an unofficially marked, semi-bushwhack heads off for approximately another 1.5 mi. (2.4 km) to the summit of Erebus Mountain. If you decide to take this side trip to Bumps Pond Lookout, be sure to take the fork which angles up the slope to the right. Avoid the horse trail which stays on the level.

The main trail continues northward. A shortcut through the neck of a road curve makes a nice place to rest. A large log marks the location of what was once a very nice spring. It needs to be cleaned out and is not recommended for drinking from at this time.

The red marked trail ends at 4.2 mi. (6.8 km), where it again meets the yellow marked trail which comes down off Sleeping Beauty Mountain. This is the trail up the mountain that you should take on the return trip.

Bumps Pond Outlet is followed for a brief span. Considerable beaver activity is noted. Following yellow markers, a gradual descent occurs until you pass through a small hollow. Then the slope becomes moderate and remains so until Fishbrook Pond is reached.

Almost before you realize you are there, both Fishbrook Pond and its first lean-to appear at 5.2 mi. (8.4 km). The setting is most attractive. Firewood is scarce, however, and you are advised to pack in a camp stove if you plan to camp there.

Directly across the pond, a second lean-to stands alone on a picturesque open point. The trail to it leads around the east shoreline of the pond. The pond's outlet is crossed by a bridge not far from the first lean-to. At the northern end of the pond a major trail junction is located at 5.6 mi. (9.1 km). Turning left (west), the second lean-to is 0.1 mi. (0.2 km) along the red marked trail.

Trails north of the junction are described below in the Black Mountain and South Loop section. The red trail west heads down to Black Mountain Point on Lake George.

DAY 2

For the return trip, backtrack 1.4 mi. (2.3 km) to the yellow marked trail up Sleeping Beauty Mountain, which drops off the shoulder of the road at Bumps Pond Outlet (0.0 mi.). The climb from this route is very easy and should not be missed.

Crossing the outlet on top of a beaver dam, you can see several dams in the direction of the pond. The trail then climbs gradually towards the summit. Several switchbacks are negotiated and the trail becomes a moderate grade. When the leaves are off the trees, fairly good views to the east are available near the summit. The trail passes just beneath the wooded peak at approximately 0.5 mi. (0.8 km). From here it descends slightly and continues along the ridge with comfortable ups and downs.

After another ten minutes of walking, a trail joins at an acute angle from the left. There is no sign, but small arrows have been carved into the trees. Continue straight ahead. The trail climbs gradually for another 100 yds. (92 m), where it terminates at the open lookout from which a marvelous view is seen. The lookout is at the 1.1 mi. (1.8 km) point.

To the southeast is seen a wide straight valley, leading straight to Fort Ann. Glacial Lake Vermont once connected Lake Champlain with points south, and this unusual Adirondack valley remains as a remnant of the past. Just to its right is Mount Hope. The highest mountain to the south of you is Buck Mountain. Further right to the southwest is Little Buck Mountain. Lake George stretches out before you to the east, with Bolton Landing on the distant shore. Shelving Rock Mountain, like an inverted soup bowl, is due east of you. Northwest Bay goes behind the Tongue Mountain Range across the lake. Crane Mountain stands out with its flat top in the distant southwest. The Adirondack high peaks are seen over the Tongue Mountain Range to the northwest. If you move around to the extreme left of the lookout you can see northeastward into the mountains of Vermont.

To descend the mountain, return 0.1 mi. (0.2 km) to the trail junction you passed just before reaching the lookout. The trail to the right drops down a moderate grade through a series of switchbacks. You curve around, finally arriving directly below the steep cliffs of the lookout. These rocks are most impressive. The stonework seen at various points was originally built to make the trail passable for horses, though this route is not suitable for equestrians today. The junction is reached after walking 1.2 mi. (1.9 km), making the whole Sleeping Beauty trail a total of 2.3 mi. (3.7 km). From this junction you return along the same route you came in on for another 3.4 mi. (5.5 km) to the Shelving Rock Road parking area.

Black Mountain and South Loop

Difficulty: Moderate to difficult
Round Trip Distance: 14.2 mi. (23.0 km)
Time Necessary: 2 days
Map: Bolton Landing 15′ Series

The trailhead (0.0 mi.) is at the rear of the Huletts Landing DEC parking area on Pike Brook Road. Climbing a short distance, you almost immediately reach a dirt road. Turn left (west) and follow it and red trail markers 0.9 mi. (1.5 km) to a junction with a DEC sign post. The fire tower on Black Mountain can be seen from this point.

Leaving the dirt road, your trail forks to the right and skirts some private property. Stay to the trail here. The smaller woods road has a gradual grade and passes through attractive hardwoods. Continue to follow red foot trail markers. Ignore the larger snowmobile markers, which you will also see.

Another junction is reached at 1.3 mi. (2.1 km). A sign on a tree indicates the direction to Lapland Pond. Turn left (south) here and begin an easy descent which ends at a bridge over a pretty brook.

Crossing the brook, you regain some of the lost elevation as you follow a stream up a valley. A small sign on a tree at the 2.2 mi. (3.6 km) point indicates you have reached the junction, where a side trail leads 0.2 mi. (0.3 km) to the lean-to at Lapland Pond. This side trail bears left, crosses a small stream, and winds around the east side of the pond. There may be some difficulty following the trail in places, but if you keep to the edge of the pond you'll soon arrive at the lean-to.

Lapland Pond is very appealing, though heavily used. Sitting high above the pond, a sloping rock massif slants down to the water's edge. As on most ponds in this region, a beaver house is seen and birdlife abounds. The heavily occupied lean-to has little firewood available. You are reminded that only dead and down wood may be chopped up for firewood. A camp stove is advisable.

From the Lapland Pond lean-to side trail junction it is only 0.2 mi. (0.3 km) to a major trail crossing. At 2.4 mi. (3.9 km) this trail intersection has a yellow marked route that bears right in the direction of Round Pond. Yellow markers also bear left and head south to Milman Pond. Some care has to be taken here, since the trail junction is swampy and the signs seem to be scattered about in a somewhat random fashion.

The path to Milman Pond hugs the west side of Lapland Pond. This section of trail is truly a woods path, and one must keep track of the trail markers. A stream is crossed where beaver runs make it seem the trail bears right. However, the correct way swings left around the flooded section.

At about 3.0 mi. (4.9 km) a snowmobile trail is reached at a T-intersection. Turn right (west) and follow it up a moderate grade to a small stream crossing. Take care not to continue up the grade along the snowmobile route, once across the stream. Instead, the hiking trail abruptly turns left and follows the stream uphill.

Leveling off at the top of the rise, you see Milman Pond below you to the right. Before long, you drop down toward the water and at 4.3 mi. (7.0 km) reach the Milman Pond lean-to. This is a newer type lean-to, which was precut and air-dropped into the site. It's interesting to compare lean-to styles; although they all appear alike at first glance, you'll see the personal mark of the builder in the details of each structure. An experienced hiker can often tell you, simply from these details, who built a particular lean-to.

The terrain changes after leaving Milman Pond. Passing over a ridge line, the woods open somewhat. You follow a land contour for awhile; then you climb over the divide and gradually lose elevation as you approach Fishbrook Pond. The more open forest is a nice variation in scenery.

Greenland Pond junction is reached at 5.3 mi. (8.6 km). This side trail follows red trail markers northeastward for 1.0 mi. (1.6 km) to the north end of Greenland Pond. From there a less maintained path strikes northward to intersect the snowmobile trail, east of where the Lapland Pond trail cuts into it.

The yellow marked trail you have been following continues 0.3 mi. (0.5 km) southward to another junction. It appears that the trail would go straight ahead, but it doesn't. Instead it drops diagonally down a slope to the right to the shore of Fishbrook Pond, where there is a major junction at the 5.6 mi. (9.1 km) point.

A red marked foot trail leads 0.2 mi. (0.3 km) around the north shore to a lean-to which sits out on an open point. The yellow marked foot trail proceeds southward along the east shoreline. At 5.9 mi. (9.6 km) Fishbrook Pond Outlet is crossed on a bridge. Still following the shoreline, you reach a second lean-to at 6.0 mi. (9.7 km).

DAY 2

Fishbrook Pond makes an ideal camping area from which several possible trips can originate.

The route suggested here returns 3.6 mi. (5.8 km) to the junction described at the 2.4 mi. (3.9 km) mark. Using this junction as a starting point (0.0 mi.), a return route to the Pike Brook Road parking area is possible by circling the base and then ascending over Black Mountain.

The yellow trail turns westward from this junction, passing over a small divide to Round Pond, which appears after 0.3 mi. (0.5 km) of walking. Another small rise is broached before you drop down to Black Mountain Pond at 0.7 mi. (1.1 km). On its north shore, several meters upslope from the shore, a nice lean-to keeps watch over this little jewel of water.

Continuing eastward another 0.3 mi. (0.5 km), the trail junction from Black Mountain Point on Lake George joins your route. To the left, a red trail descends 1400 ft. (428 m) in 2.0 mi. (3.2 km) to the lake shore.

The way to the summit of Black Mountain swings uphill to the right, past this intersection, and follows red trail markers. You encounter several switchbacks as the moderate grade steepens. You will gain 936 ft. (286 m) in elevation before reaching the fire tower at its peak. Views of Lake George soon begin to appear. The summit is reached at 1.8 mi. (2.9 km), and there are vistas in all directions. Tongue Mountain Range is directly across the lake, with the Adirondack high peaks beyond. Lake Champlain's South Bay and Vermont are to the northeast. Almost the entire length of Lake George's 32 mi. (51.8 km) are visible from this summit. Summit elevation is 2646 ft. (809 m).

It is 2.8 mi. (4.5 km) from the top of Black Mountain back to the Pike Brook Road parking area. The trail descends past the fire observer's cabin and then enters the woods to the east. A short steep rock face is negotiated before the trail moderates to a more relaxing rate of descent. A pleasant woods road, which passes a rushing stream and then a quiet spring, is soon reached on the left.

At 3.3 mi. (5.3 km) the Lapland Pond junction is reached. It comes in from the right. From here it is 1.3 mi. (2.1 km) back to the parking area. At 4.6 mi. (7.5 km), a right hand turn takes you down the brief slope to the parking area.

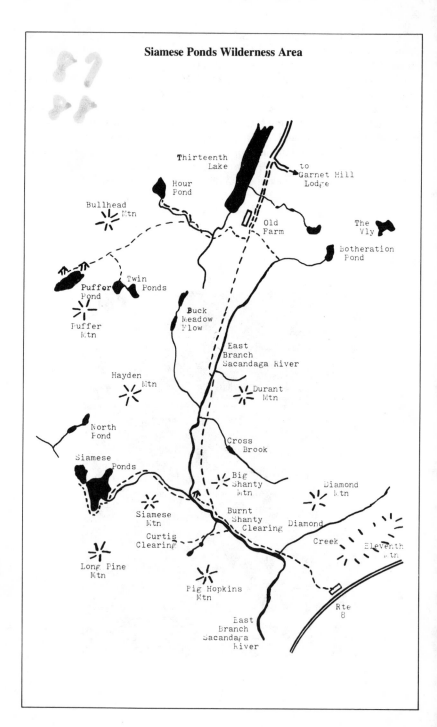

Siamese Ponds Wilderness Area

Thirteenth
Lake

to
Garnet Hill
Lodge

Hour
Pond

Bullhead
Mtn

Old
Farm

The
Vly

Botheration
Pond

Twin
Ponds

Puffer
Pond

Buck
Meadow
Flow

East
Branch
Sacandaga River

Puffer
Mtn

Hayden
Mtn

Durant
Mtn

North
Pond

Cross
Brook

Siamese
Ponds

Big
Shanty
Mtn

Diamond
Mtn

Siamese
Mtn

Burnt
Shanty
Clearing

Diamond

Curtis
Clearing

Creek

Eleventh
Mtn

Long Pine
Mtn

Pig Hopkins
Mtn

Rte
8

East
Branch
Sacandaga
River

3. The Siamese Ponds Wilderness Area

Much of the Forest Preserve approximates true wilderness more today than it did a century ago: the trails by which we now enter and enjoy this returning wilderness were created by man's original encroachment.

The early lumbermen bought huge land tracts for only a few cents an acre, raped the forest, and abandoned the land. For refusal to pay taxes, the state eventually reclaimed these sites. Homesteaders who had purchased cleared land from lumbermen found the short growing season and thin topsoil of the North Country difficult, and frequently gave up their inholdings and left.

Time has replaced the forests so abused by the early lumber kings. Natural tree successions are gradually returning the woods to its original state. The scars of the past are slowly being obliterated.

The Siamese Ponds Wilderness Area is part of this Forest Preserve. The Siamese Ponds trail follows much of the old stage coach road Bill Wakely talked the state into building from North Creek to Baker's Mills. The trail heading west from Old Farm Clearing was the main route to Indian Lake in the 1840s. Only the unexpected presence of apple blossoms in the spring of the year remain to remind us that Burnt Shanty Clearing was once a homestead. Curtis Clearing, Hayden Mountain, Hayes Flow, and Big Hopkins Mountain give clues as to whom we might have met a century ago in this country. Botheration Pond, Balm of Gilead Mountain, Ruby Mountain, Chatiemac Lake, and the Kunjamuk all suggest things about the kinds of people they were. For a brief time man intruded and then stole away, leaving only names to entice the curious to ponder bygone days.

Buildings burn down, corduroy rots, hayfields become deer meadows, and memories fade as the shadows of time lengthen and blur man's perceptions of the past. Only the old roads remain to provide us entry into this land and back to another era. Without them, few people would venture here to witness the return of wilderness. Perhaps man's temporary intrusion had a purpose that was unknown to the intruders in their time.

The Siamese Ponds Wilderness Area has numerous trails and endless bushwhacking possibilities. Sprinkled among the over 100,000 acres of rolling hills are a few mountains of the 3000 ft. (917 m) class and many smaller summits and bumps. Sixty-seven bodies of water are found here.

See the Adirondack Mountain Club's *Guide to Adirondack Trails: Central Region,* by Bruce Wadsworth, for a comprehensive description of the Siamese Ponds Wilderness Area. The ADK map "Trails of the Central Region" might also be useful.

The Siamese Ponds Trail

Difficulty: Easy, with a few long challenging grades
Round Trip Distance: 12.6 mi. (20.4 km)
Time Necessary: 2 days
Map: Thirteenth Lake 15' Series

The Siamese Ponds Trail provides a variety of terrain and beauty that should satisfy any backpacker. The beginner will find a generally easy route with enough hardships at times to make him aware that easy is a relative term. The experienced trekker will recognize the inifinite possibilities for side trips, fishing, and nature study. The more hearty types can step off the trail at almost any point to be swallowed up in true wilderness isolation, where only the experienced should venture. Cross-country skiers and snowshoers find this a winter wonderland. Skiiers usually make the run south from Thirteenth Lake to Rte. 8. It's a good day's through trip, with the last long down grade for the expert class only. The rest of the trip is relatively easy, though long. Spring snow lasts a long time here.

The trailhead is on the west side of Rte. 8, 4.0 mi. (6.5 km) south of Baker's Mills. A large wooden DEC signpost marks the spacious parking area. (Be sure to examine the older metal Forest Preserve signpost located at the opposite side of the parking area.) Trailhead elevation is 1760 ft. (538 m). Blue foot trail markers and yellow ski markers lead you up a trail at the rear of the parking area. The well constructed shelter protecting the trail register is the first of many indicators that this is a very well maintained trail.

Gradual grades soon steepen as you circle up to the saddle crossing the ridge that constitutes Eleventh Mountain. Beginning so early in the hike, this fifteen minute ascent clearly informs you of your physical condition. The 0.3 mi. (0.5 km) distance gains 240 ft. (73 m) elevation.

Near the top of the grade, you may notice an old road merging with your trail from the left. This is a remnant of the old stage coach road from Baker's Mills to North Creek. The welcome easy grades you'll follow to the Sacandaga lean-to pretty much stay to this highway of the past.

A long gradual descent ensues through hardwoods. At 1.5 mi. (2.4 km) you reach the Diamond Brook bridge, where Diamond Brook flows off Diamond Mountain through a wide flat area. This is usually a rough place to get past in the spring, when meltwaters overflow the stream channel. Bear left and you'll soon pick up the trail again. You also reach the East Branch of the Sacandaga River. This most pleasant stream will occupy your attention as you follow along its left bank, walking upstream. Soon you reach a beaver meadow where you can look northward to the diamond shaped mountain from whence Diamond Brook gets its name.

The almost grown-in Burnt Shanty Clearing is reached at 2.7 mi. (4.4 km). The trail continues to parallel the East Branch of the Sacandaga, though sight of it is not quite as frequent now. The almost level route gives you much opportunity to enjoy your surroundings.

There is a trail junction at 3.5 mi. (5.7 km). The right fork leads another 5.5 mi. (8.9 km) to Old Farm Clearing and Thirteenth Lake.

Take the left fork. It leads 0.5 mi. (0.8 km) to the Sacandaga lean-to, where a bridge crosses over the East Branch of the Sacandaga. This is a most attractive place. The lean-to sits on a flat area a few feet above the river surface, giving you a commanding view of the waterway and points northward. The breezes emanating from the river provide a welcome sensation as you sit on the lean-to's deacon seat, drinking in the rewarding sights along with some of the cool river water.

The bridge is somewhat of an enigma. It is a beautiful suspension bridge, airlifted to its present location in 1967. It is clearly needed here. However, concrete and steel in a wilderness area make the believer of true wilderness ethics blush with chagrin. The best that one can do is to say it is the exception that proves the rule.

The neophyte hiker who is all tuckered out will probably decide this is about as idyllic a spot to stay as can be found, and will leave Siamese Ponds for a packless side trip before heading back out the next morning.

Siamese Ponds lies 2.3 mi. (3.7 km) to the west, across the bridge. As you hike along, you are at first so occupied with the glimpses of beaver activity seen through the trees at your right that you don't notice that you're gaining elevation. The rolling terrain slowly rises as you skirt the lower shoulder of Siamese Mountain. Siamese Brook is the large stream that you cross after about fifteen minutes walking. It's a good place for a refreshing drink. Before height of land is reached at about the 6.0 mi. (10.0 km) point, over 425 ft. (130 m) elevation is gained.

Siamese Ponds is soon seen below you to the right. A good campsite is passed just before you reach the shoreline, where a second, smaller site is found at the shoreline of the lower pond. This is a very pretty sheet of water. At times, a strong breeze is felt as the fetch wind whips down the pond's distance. It's the sort of place where you want to sit awhile and perhaps watch the birds flit over the water as the clouds drift by overhead. You might be tempted to throw out a fishing line as an excuse to remain there reading a book for the rest of the day.

It would be best to camp at one of the previously mentioned locations. However, a hike to the upper pond is encouraged because it will strikingly illustrate what beavers can do to an ecosystem. Crossing the pond's outlet, walk along the very edge of the west shoreline, following a narrow path. As beavers have methodically dammed up the outlet of the lower pond, the pond has progressively enlarged. By early summer 1980, the rim had just about overflowed.

You'll enjoy the long descent on the way back to the Sacandaga lean-to. Allow plenty of time, however, for regaining the 400 ft. (122 m) elevation that you lost between Diamond Brook and the col on Eleventh Mountain. Look for the cliffs as you begin this climb. Then keep an eye out for where the old stage coach road branches off to the right as you drop down the far side of the col towards the parking area.

Suspension Bridge on East Sacandaga River

Puffer Pond

Difficulty: Easy, with minor grades.
Round Trip Distance: 8.6 mi. (13.9 km)
Time Necessary: 2 days
Map: Thirteenth Lake 15′ Series

Puffer Pond is ideal for a backpacker's beginning hike. The grades are short, the trail is excellent, and the country can not be surpassed. More experienced hikers may do this outing as a day hike or extend it with a side trip into Hour Pond. With a waiting vehicle at the other end of the line, Puffer Pond can be the first night's destination on a through trip to Kings Flow or John Pond.

Fine ski touring and snowshoeing is found on trails originating at this trailhead. The Puffer Pond trail requires a few stream crossings that should be easy in late winter. A through trip of about 11.0 mi. (17.8 km) to the Rte. 8 Siamese Wilderness trailhead near Baker's Mills is also frequently done, but requires expert skill in one last section just before arriving at Rte. 8.

Trailhead access is off Rte. 28 at North River. A sign points the way to Siamese Ponds Wilderness Area. A blacktop road takes you 4.2 mi. (6.8 km) to a road fork. (Do not turn at the earlier fork for Thirteenth Lake.) A small sign indicates you should bear right here, on a good dirt road which is not plowed beyond this point in winter. Another 2.0 mi. (3.2 km) of driving brings you to the Old Farm Clearing, which is the trailhead. This old farmstead of the 1870s is now the site of a large tree plantation. Abundant parking and a DEC trail register are located here.

The trail starts at the rear of the parking area (0.0 mi.). Immediately to the left is the trail heading to Botheration Pond. Just beyond, a spring is found at the left of the trail. Walking through the tree plantation, a DEC signpost is reached at 0.1 mi. (0.2 km). Take the right fork and continue through the plantation, following blue DEC trail markers.

A few minutes later you come to a climax forest and begin a gradual descent. A major inlet of Thirteenth Lake is crossed at 1.0 mi. (1.6 km). From this low point of 1700 ft. (520 m) elevation, you will gain approximately 484 ft. (148 m) before reaching Puffer Pond.

A moderate grade develops and you head upslope. You won't travel far before the sounds of cascading water are heard. Soon, you see the outlet of Hour Brook below you to the right. With its bubbling waters to entertain you, a col is quickly reached, the trail levels, and you cross Hour Pond Brook.

Turning left, you continue on the level beside the brook until a little rise brings you to a side trail on the right at 1.4 mi. (2.3 km). This side trail leads 2.0 mi. (3.2 km) to Hour Pond.

Still following the brook, you almost immediately reach a second crossing place. Hour Brook makes a horseshoe turn, cutting through large rocks and forming a pretty little water slide. This is a good place to take a break and enjoy your surroundings.

Once across the brook, rolling terrain is encountered, with each new roll a bit higher than the last one. The magnificent beech, maple, and hemlock forest in this region has a number of immense trees that come close to three feet in diameter.

Descending one of the humps at 1.9 mi. (3.1 km), you cross a small wet section on corduroy. (You may have to leave the trail here and circle to the right.) At 2.2 mi. (3.6 km) a beaver meadow is seen. Here, an abandoned beaver dam has broken down. The once impressive pond behind the dam has become a lovely meadow where deer doubtless abound in the dusk of evening.

Another log bridge takes you across this tributary of Hour Pond Brook. You plunge back into the woods. Summer flowers, lush ferns, hammering woodpeckers, and an occasional chattering chipmunk keep your interest as you proceed through this enjoyable forest. Then, rather suddenly, you arrive at Puffer Pond and the little side trail that leads to the first lean-to at 4.0 mi. (6.5 km).

Located at the northeast end of Puffer Pond, the lean-to looks out across the pond to the steep slopes of Puffer Mountain. A path from the lean-to soon rejoins the main trail, which follows the north shoreline. Along the way two nice campsites are passed. A murky spring is seen just before the second lean-to is reached at 4.3 mi. (7.0 km). This lean-to sits well above the water's edge near the midpoint of the pond. From it, the trail swings northward to Kings Flow and John Pond.

4. The Wilcox Lake Wild Forest Area

The Wilcox Lake Wild Forest Area is little known and much neglected by hikers. Hunters, fishermen, and snowmobilers frequent the area, but it is deserted for much of the summer. Once far more populated than it is today, a network of roads traverses the region. Some are still open to vehicles, but many now exist only as foot trails. The Oregon Trail connected the little hamlet of Oregon with Bakertown and points south.

Countless ponds and mountains dot the region, whetting one's curiosity with their strange names. Cod Pond, Lixard Pond, Bearpen Peak, Winona Lake, and Seneca Mountain are but a few of them.

Lixard Pond via the Oregon Trail

Difficulty: Easy, with woods knowledge.
Round Trip Distance: 16.8 mi. (27.2 km)
Time Necessary: 2 days
Maps: Thirteenth Lake 15′ Series
** Harrisburg 15′ Series**

This trip is interesting because of the variety of trail conditions you encounter. It is highly recommended for the woods-wise backpacker. The beginner should chalk up a few more simple trips before tackling this one. The terrain makes walking a pleasure. Much of the route is on the Oregon Trail and other old roads. You may go a mile or more between trail markers, will have one tricky stream crossing, and will find a few sections that bear no resemblance at all to the hiking highways of the High Peaks. None of this, however, should hinder one who knows how to read terrain and feels at ease in the woods. The quantity and variety of wildlife in this region are truly astounding. The trees are often immense.

Trailhead access is off the east side of Rte. 8. Turn onto Rte. 8 from Rte. 30, 3.0 mi. (4.9 km) north of Wells. Drive 10.1 mi. (16.4 km) towards Wevertown, where the well marked Shanty Brook trailhead and parking area is located. If approaching from Wevertown, Shanty Brook trailhead is 4.4 mi. (7.1 km) south of the Siamese Ponds trailhead. There is a privy uphill from the rear of the parking area.

The trail begins at the south end of the parking area (0.0 mi.), where a sign for North Bend is found. Follow snowmobile markers along this relatively new section of trail, which leads up a gradual, stony grade. Soon it descends to a bridge crossing at Stewart Creek at 0.6 mi. (1.0 km). Avoid the unmarked trail to the right just before the bridge. After crossing the bridge, make a short climb to the Cod Pond trail junction at 0.7 mi. (1.1 km).

Turn left at this junction. The walk from here to Cod Pond Flow is delightful. The level trail reaches a small beaver dam across Stewart Creek at 1.6 mi. (2.6

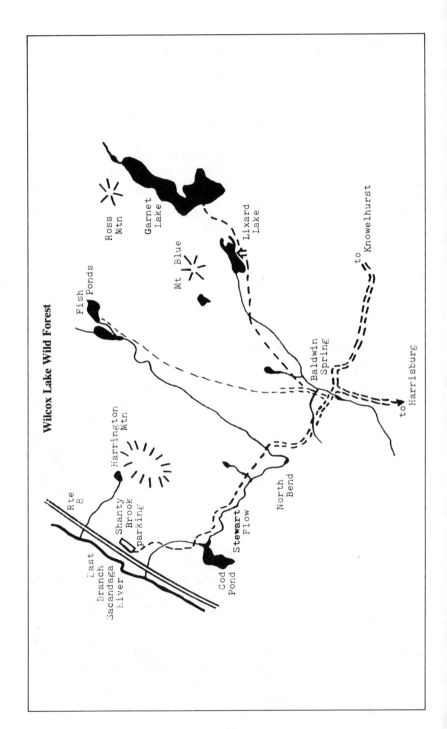

Wilcox Lake Wild Forest

km). Here, a path leads to the pretty little pond behind the dam. At 1.7 mi. (2.8 km) the wide bridge over the outlet of Cod Pond Flow is reached. Downstream, the water cuts through an angular rock formation to the beaver pond below. Above the bridge, lush Cod Pond Flow stretches before you. Birds, varying from cedar waxwings to great blue herons, are evident here.

The trail stays upslope from the water. Traveling eastward, you pass a huge boulder field of glacial erratics. At about 2.1 mi. (3.4 km) the snowmobile trail makes a turn and drops down to the wet meadowlands along Stewart Creek. Some 30 yds. (28 m) upslope from the opening to the meadows a side trail to the left is seen. By taking this left fork you can stay on high ground and keep dry. This route is easy to follow, but has only a few red ribbons for markers. It eventually rejoins the snowmobile trail.

At 2.6 mi. (4.2 km) you emerge from the woods into a wide grassy vlei, through which a single, deep but narrow tributary of Stewart Creek flows. A large beaver house built against a boulder in the stream draws your attention. A few yards upstream from the beaver house some logs have been placed across the stream. It will be necessary to walk around to your left to reach them. This little crossing courts disaster for the unwary. It might be worth a few minutes time to collect a couple more logs to both strengthen and enlarge the crossing surface. Once across the vlei, swing back to your right and connect up with the snowmobile trail, seen coming in off the meadows, again.

Continue southward through primitive forests. There are few markers and the trail is narrow. Occasional blowdowns must be circumvented, but the trail is generally obvious. Sign of all manner of wildlife is abundant here. At 3.3 mi. (5.3 km) you again descend slightly to another stream. This is Stewart Creek and you are at North Bend. Here, the stream is wide but very shallow. Downstream, Stewart Creek has made a 180-degree horseshoe turn towards its source at Fish Ponds. Hence, the name North Bend. A beaver dam has been started a short distance upstream. In summer it is so shallow that you may just wade across, stepping from rock to rock. In any event, this crossing presents no obstacle except during spring meltoffs.

Once across Stewart Creek, a wider path takes you to a clearing at 3.4 mi. (5.5 km). This is a major turnaround for snowmobilers. At the north side of the clearing a trail heads 3.1 mi. (5.0 km) to Fish Ponds. A privy is located near this point.

The character of the terrain changes rapidly as you leave this clearing. It is evident that vehicles frequent the wide woods road you are now following, but the change isn't too disturbing. Spruce and immense balsams appear. Your rate of travel increases and, as you swing to the east, you negotiate a slight up-hill grade.

Height of land brings you to a junction at approximately 4.4 mi. (7.1 km). Avoid the unmarked turn to the right. Following snowmobile markers to the left, you begin a long gradual descent to Baldwin Springs. Stay on the heavily used route whenever occasional side routes are seen. A few minutes below height of land a large attractive flooded beaver pond is seen on your right. One last drop brings you to Baldwin Springs at 5.1 mi. (8.3 km).

Baldwin Springs is a very interesting sand flat. Sterile sand encourages a different type of tree growth from what you have been seeing. Numerous tamaracks and tapering spruces are slowly filling in the plains. Most trees are small; the viewer can see the distant mountains and has a sense of perspective quite different from that one gains while walking through dense forest. The old spring still provides cold fresh water.

From the DEC register at the trail junction in the clearing, a well used dirt road, West Stony Creek Road, is to the right. It leads south and soon hooks up with the old road to Harrisburg Lake.

The route you want turns northward (to the left). It is much less used and immediately crosses East Stony Creek. At 5.3 mi. (8.6 km) you come to a junction. The trail to Fish Ponds is straight ahead.

Turn right at this junction. Recent sign makers have turned Lixard Pond into "Lizard Pond," so follow the incorrectly labeled signs from this point onward. The woods road is grassy and bears a few wheel ruts. At 6.0 mi. (9.7 km) you reach the Indian Pond trail junction. This little used trail swings to the right.

Turn left at this junction. You begin an easy, almost unnoticed upgrade which will continue all the way to Lixard Pond. You'll soon notice an unusual area below you to the right. It is seasonally flooded, but is more of a muddy morass in the summer. Ferns and grasses grow high on the snowmobile trail you are following, but there is no difficulty finding your way.

At approximately 7.9 mi. (12.8 km), two bridges take you over the almost dry outlet of Lixard Pond. The western end of the pond is reached at 8.2 mi. (13.3 km). Five more minutes of walking along the attractive pond's shoreline brings you to the lean-to at 8.4 mi. (13.6 km).

Lixard Pond lean-to is used primarily by snowmobilers, who come across the frozen ice of Garnet Lake 1.0 mi. (1.6 km) further along the trail north of the lean-to. It receives almost no use in the summer. Set a few feet back from the water's edge under the trees, it looks out at Mount Blue directly across the pond.

The splendid view from Mount Blue's summit makes a climb to its top worth spending an extra day at the pond. To make this easy bushwhack, continue on the trail towards Garnet Lake. A height of land will be reached after traveling about 0.5 mi. (0.8 km). Take a northwest compass bearing and follow the ridge upward. Ascent is about 1200 ft. (367 m) to an elevation of 2950 ft. (902 m).

The bare cliffs of Crane Mountain are seen in the distance beyond the east end of Lixard Pond. Crane Mountain's fire tower can be seen (1980) on the southeast end of the summit. This is one of the most impressive views of Crane Mountain to be found.

Wilcox Lake

Difficulty: Easy
Round Trip Distance: 10.0 mi. (16.2 km)
Time: 2 days
Map: Harrisburg 15′ Series

This is an interesting trip along old logging trails through a maturing mixed wood forest. Much of the route follows the left bank of East Stony Creek. It is the kind of outing that shouldn't be hurried. Flowers abound along the streams, deer are frequently seen, and Canadian geese stop over at Wilcox Lake during their migrations. Take your time and enjoy the surroundings.

Access to the trailhead is off Rte. 30 on the southern edge of the hamlet of Hope. If approaching from the direction of the Great Sacandaga Lake, turn east onto Creek Road 3.2 mi. (5.2 km) north of the DEC signpost for the Benson Section of the Northville-Placid Trail. There is a family cemetery plot at the Creek Road intersection. Drive along Creek Road 2.8 mi. (4.5 km) until you reach a road fork, where DEC signs are located. Turn left onto Mud Creek Road. It will become a dirt road after a few miles. A DEC signpost at the trailhead on East Stony Creek is seen on the left after driving 4.9 mi. (7.9 km). Park off the road, but avoid proceeding onto the Brownell Camp property, which is privately owned. Brownell's Camp has a long history as one of the early hunters' hotels in the woods.

From the signpost (0.0 mi.) the trail passes through private property following blue trail markers. The route you are following is a snowmobile trail in the winter, so the bridges are well constructed. Tenant Creek is crossed on one such bridge. Thereafter, you move away from streams but return to the banks of East Stony Creek at 1.0 mi. (1.6 km).

Turning right, you follow an old logging road along the left bank of East Stony Creek for almost 3.0 mi. (4.9 km). The stream is broad and moves with considerable force in the springtime. Great blocks of ice are pushed up on the shores. In summer, however, it presents a tranquil scene, with long-stemmed flowers poking through the green ferns which cloak the banks.

The grade increases at about 2.2 mi. (3.6 km), but the walking is so comfortable you don't really mind. You move away from the stream and begin to notice more conifers as elevation is gained. At just about height of land you pass out of Hamilton County and into Warren County. Gradual grades take you back downward to Dayton Creek, which is crossed on a bridge at 3.1 mi. (5.0 km). There is a fork in the trail just beyond Dayton Creek. Take the left side of the fork, which returns you to the bank of East Stony Creek.

At 3.8 mi. (6.2 km) you come to a wide metal suspension bridge that spans East Stony Creek. This is a good lunch spot, with ducks often seen dashing along the surface of the water. Cross the bridge and carefully follow yellow snowmobile trail markers.

The trail narrows and you climb a moderate grade over the northern shoulder of Wilcox Mountain. Many fallen trees give evidence of violent storms in the past. Finally, height of land is reached at a trail junction at 4.3 mi. (7.0 km), having gained 250 ft. (76 m) elevation. Here the left-hand branch of the junction heads southeastward 4.5 mi. (7.3 km) to Willis Lake.

Turn right and head north. A jeep trail enters from the right, 0.1 mi. (0.2 km) further along the trail. An informal campsite is found at this point. Continuing straight ahead you find a barrier marking the endpoint for vehicular travel, but irresponsible individuals sometimes drive on to the lake, anyway. Deep ruts are dug into the steep slope. Fortunately this last section is very short. A moderately steep grade drops down to the shore of Wilcox Lake, which is reached at 4.8 mi. (7.8 km).

Woods Road to Murphy Lake

A DEC trail register is at the shoreline. The lake's expanse is before you, with surrounding hills casting a green sheen over the water. Two lean-tos are located on this lake. The first is 0.1 mi. (0.2 km) around the south side of the lake. It sits up above the water, the surface elevation of which is 1445 ft. (442 m). The second lean-to is to the left of the trail register, 0.2 mi. (0.3 km) around the west shoreline. It is on a small point and has several informal campsites at varying distances behind the lean-to. This second shelter is perhaps the nicer of the two shelters.

Bennett, Middle, and Murphy Lakes

Difficulty: Easy with some moderate grades.
Round Trip Distance: 6.2 mi. (10.0 km)
Time Necessary: 2 days
Map: Harrisburg 15′ Series

The route followed on this outing has existed since the early 1800s. They were still paying bounties on wolves in 1826 in the town of Hope, but boom days were ahead. Lumbering, tanning, sheep raising, and farming generated a number of thriving communities from the 1840s through the Civil War period. Then things began to slow down and the forest started to close in again. Today, the old route to Murphy Lake and Pumpkin Hollow is a snowmobile trail where old building foundations and stone walls give silent testimony to another era.

There is an attractive lean-to at Murphy Lake from which bushwhacks up surrounding peaks can easily be made. The trip is relatively short, leaving ample time for enjoying the lakes along your trail. It is a pleasant trip which gains 540 ft. (165 m) in elevation before arriving at Murphy Lake.

Access to the trailhead is from Rte. 30 on the southern edge of the hamlet of Hope. If approaching from the direction of the Great Sacandaga Lake, turn east onto Creek Road 3.2 mi. (5.2 km) north of the DEC signpost for the Benson Section of the Northville-Placid Trail. There is a family cemetery plot at the Creek Road intersection. Drive along Creek Road 2.6 mi. (4.2 km) to the trailhead. As you descend a grade, the DEC trail sign is on the left side of the road.

Yellow foot trail markers and red snowmobile markers guide your way. The grade upwards is steady. The route is rocky. After about fifteen minutes, it levels somewhat but still has a gradual slope. There is evidence of lumbering in the recent past.

The trail stays above the west side of Bennett Lake, but you catch glimpses of it through the trees as you approach it. At 1.2 mi. (1.9 km) an unmarked trail forks to the right. It drops downward 0.1 mi. (0.2 km) to the sandy shore of Bennett Lake. An informal campsite is found here; this would be a good spot for a last swim on the return trip.

From the junction, the route soon begins to climb over a ridge. The increased steepness has caused vehicles traveling this route to dig up the trail quite a bit. In spite of this, the character of the forest becomes more wild. Height of land is reached at 1.7 mi. (2.8 km), and the way levels for a stretch before climbing again. At 2.2 mi. (3.6 km) the route resumes level going and stays pretty much on the contour as you walk beside a brook. The trail swings above the west side of Middle Lake. At approximately 2.6 mi. (4.2 km) an unmarked side trail leads a short distance to the shore of Middle Lake.

There is an informal campsite of sorts located here. Pickerel weed, with long purple spikes, and various lilies line the bank of this dark body of water. An island presents itself, and the distant shore has cliffs behind it. Middle Lake is quite charming.

The trail to Murphy Lake is almost level, actually descending 20 ft. (6 m) along the way. The southern end of the lake is a short fifteen minutes beyond Middle Lake. After a brief walk along the east side of Murphy Lake, the lean-to is reached at 3.1 mi. (5.0 km).

The lean-to sits in a handsome grouping of hemlocks near the water. Small mountains surround the lake. Lily pads decorate its surface. The trail continues around the north end of the lake past the lean-to.

It is another 3.0 mi. (4.9 km) to Pumpkin Hollow, where a 1.7 mi. (2.8 km) drive from that trailhead will take you back to Rte. 30. If two cars are available, you may prefer a through trip. The trailhead in Pumpkin Hollow is found at the right side of a curve in the road on a small grade. A maroon-colored house (1980) is opposite the trailhead. A pulloff for parking is just a bit further around the curve.

A small valley runs nearly north from the north end of the lake. Bushwhacks can be made up either of the small mountains at that end of the lake by following the valley about 0.2 mi. (0.3 km) to a height of land some 30 ft. (9 m) above the lake level. Once past the cliff in this valley, you can ascend either to the east or the west. The eastern climb is slightly higher. Views of Moose Mountain to the northwest and Cathead Mountain to the west are your rewards for your efforts. Be careful picking your ascent and descent routes through the rocks.

5. The West Canada Lakes Wilderness Area

The West Canada Lakes Wilderness Area is the headwater source for three major rivers: The Cedar River flows into the Hudson; the Indian River supplies the Black River; and West Canada Creek empties into the Mohawk River.

A casual look at a map will indicate that, for the most part, this area is buffered by other state lands around it. The Moose River Recreation Area, Jessup River Wild Forest, West Canada Mountain Primitive Area, and the Pillsbury Lake Primitive Area are the primary bodies. The effect of this is that it is very difficult to get into the heart of this area and back out again in a two day weekend trip. Hence, the West Canada Lakes and the Cedar Lakes have remained truly wild.

It is a far cry from the old days when the Belden brothers ran their secret mine on Belden Mountain, or when Lucretia Howell lived with her parents in the caves north of Spruce Lake. French Louie probably had as many marksmen at his West Lake camp in a single season as now frequent the place in a five year span, since bush pilot operations have terminated.

Geographical isolation hasn't been enough to prevent man from influencing the life of this region, however. Today the scourge is not the slashing lumbermen or the deer-jacking hunter. It is acid rain. In general, the higher the elevation of the land, the greater will be the amount of acidified snow and rain that will fall. Much of this region is over 2500 ft. (765 m) in elevation. Significantly, this land is also downwind of the Great Lakes, a major source of the moisture from which snow and rain form. These two factors, the Great Lakes Effect and elevation, are taking their toll. In the 1880s Traume Haskell could catch thirty or more pounds of trout through the ice of Brooktrout Lake in a single afternoon. Today it is barren of life, and with it has gone the fish-eating loon. Sly Pond, Wolf Lake, and other bodies of water have suffered the same fate. So far, the West Canadas and the Cedar Lakes are holding their own.

The great visual beauty of this land together with this invisible blight are difficult to focus sharply in one's mind at the same time. Nevertheless, they exist together and compose man's most upsetting worldwide problem of the present decade. Can man control himself?

The Northville-Placid Trail weaves its way through this area. The Spruce Lake trip described in this section is along part of this trail. The Brooktrout Lake trip heads into the West Canadas from the Moose River Recreation Area near Limekiln Lake. Both are excellent introductory trips to this region and can form the basis from which more extended outings may be planned. See *Guide to Trails of the West-Central Adirondacks* (ADK) for further information.

Morning at Brooktrout Lake

Brooktrout Lake

Difficulty: Easy, with long grades
Round Trip Distance: 10.4 mi. (16.8 km)
Time Necessary: 2 days
Map: West Canada Lake 15' series

Brooktrout Lake is a beautiful body of water nestled in the midst of surrounding mountains. Since trout are no longer found here, the only visitors now are a few hunters in autumn and surprisingly few backpackers. It makes a nice weekend trip or a first night stop on a longer trek to the West Canadas.

The first half of the hike takes you up over a major ridge along an old logging road. A gentle descent makes the second half of the trip more interesting, and evidence of beaver, deer, and bear is seen.

Access to the trailhead is from the Limekiln Lake entrance of the Moose River Recreation Area. North of Inlet, turn off Rte. 28 at the large DEC sign for Limekiln Lake Public Campsite and Day Use Area. Continue by the campsite when you reach it on this road. The Moose River Recreation Area gateway is a short distance further along this road. Maps are available from the ranger at the gate.

From the gate, drive 8.6 mi. (13.9 km) along the good gravel Moose River Road to a major intersection, where the road turns left for Wakely Dam. Continue straight ahead another 3.3 mi. (5.3 km) on the Indian Lake Road to a fork. Bear right and drive another 0.9 mi. (1.5 km) on the Otter Brook Road. A trailhead parking area is located on the left side of the road at a gravel pit. Signs clearly mark the spot and all intersections.

From the cable barrier at the right rear of the parking area (0.0 mi.), the trail follows a nearly level course along a grassy old logging road. Yellow trail markers will eventually guide your way, but none will be seen for quite awhile. The first of several informal camping spots appears after a few minutes of walking as you approach the Falls Pond outlet stream.

A gradual grade that will continue at various degrees of steepness for the next 0.8 mi. (1.3 km) now begins. Along the way you will see a tremendous assemblage of hardwoods. From tamarack and small-toothed aspen to canoe birch and striped maple, a secondary growth succession is seen along the edge of the road competing with a more mature forest a few feet further into the forest.

At 1.5 mi. (2.4 km) the Falls Pond junction is reached. You may miss this junction if you're not looking for it. Falls Pond, with its informal campsite, is 0.4 mi. (0.6 km) up the side trail to the right.

As you continue straight ahead, the grade often changes but is always upward. From one open high spot the trail sweeps around a curve, giving you a fine view of the wetland grasses and spiring black spruces along Wolf Creek in the distance below you. Then you drop down a ways and pass an attractive beaver pond.

Ascending again, you cross the bridge over Wolf Creek as the rushing water shoots through a narrow flume under you. An informal campsite is located here. Some 140 yds. (128 m) further along the trail, you come to the Wolf Lake and

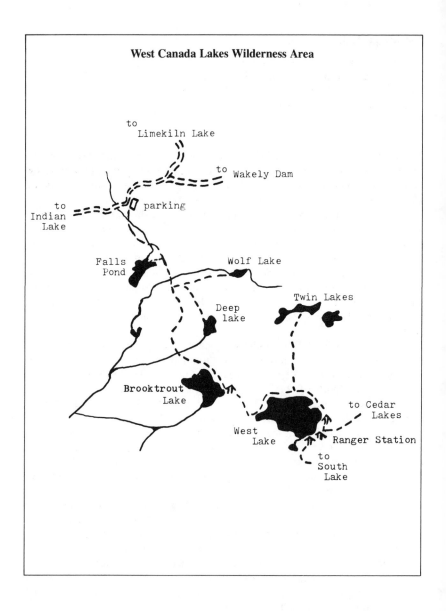

West Canada Lakes Wilderness Area

to
Limekiln Lake

to Wakely Dam

to
Indian
Lake

parking

Falls
Pond

Wolf Lake

Deep
lake

Twin Lakes

Brooktrout
Lake

to Cedar
Lakes

West
Lake

Ranger Station

to
South
Lake

Deep Lake trail junction at 2.2 mi. (3.6 km). A single side trail to these lakes heads off to the left. It forks a short distance later. Each lake is 1.0 mi. (1.6 km) from the junction.

The trail again gradually ascends over a base of glacial scoured bedrock. Finally, on a broad curve, height of land is reached. Elevation at this point is approximately 2650 ft. (810 m). You have ascended nearly 600 ft. (183 m) since leaving the parking area.

The trail now narrows and progressively becomes more of a true woods trail. A lengthy descent through occasionally draining areas of minor wetness is quite pleasant. Yellow trail markers become more evident. At 3.0 mi. (4.9 km) you skirt a beaver flooded area with an interesting low, winding dam. The trail splits at one point, but the parts soon merge again.

Mature beech, maple, yellow birch, and a few red spruce make up the forest through which you are now traveling. This region was not logged as recently as the land you saw earlier. As a result, it is more nearly a climax forest typical of this elevation.

The gradual descent goes on with a few knolls to change the pace. The outlet of Deep Lake and Twin Lakes is crossed in two parts at 3.6 mi. (5.8 km). The first part is hopped on rocks and has delicious rushing water. Over a small knoll, you cross the second part on a log bridge and turn left. A sign points the way (1980).

An easy grade takes you gradually up to a col. The trail is very comfortable here. From the top, a gradual descent takes you downward until, at 4.5 mi. (7.3 km), you pass some rock outcrops to your left. Then, a moderately steep grade takes you another 0.1 mi. (0.2 km) downward. Brooktrout Lake can be seen through the trees, but you will swing to the left and circle the northeast side of the lake several meters upslope from the shoreline.

Frequent ups and downs occur as you walk along with the lake in view. At 5.1 mi. (8.3 km) an informal campsite is passed, and the side trail to the lean-to is reached at 5.2 mi. (8.4 km).

The lean-to is located 25 yds. (23 m) off the trail to the right. It faces a large sheared-off boulder against which a fireplace is constructed. It makes a perfect heat reflector on cold, chilly nights. The lake is reached by a short path through dense spruces at the rear of the lean-to. The rock-lined shore is attractive, and the shallow water invites swimming. You are looking due west. A disappearing sun in late evening will provide the mood for a long campfire before turning in at night.

A path at the far end of the small lean-to clearing leads back to the main trail. It is another 0.7 mi. (1.1 km) of flat trail to the informal campsite on the shore of West Lake, and still another 1.8 mi. (2.9 km) along the shoreline to the ranger's cabin and two lean-tos at the west end of the lake.

Spruce Lake

Difficulty: Moderate, but a long trip.
Round Trip Distance: 20.8 mi. (33.7 km)
Time Necessary: 2 days
Maps: Piseco Lake 15′ Series
  West Canada Lakes 15′ Series

You have to walk a little to get to Spruce Lake, but it's worth the effort. This high elevation [2378 ft. (727 m)] lake provides a true wilderness experience. The trail you follow is part of the Northville-Placid Trail. From Piseco it is 38 mi. (61.6 km) through the West Canada Lakes Wilderness Area before a road is reached at Wakely Dam.

Access is off Rte. 8 in the village of Piseco. At the north end of the village, just west of the small airport, is a DEC signpost at a road junction. Following the road 0.8 mi. (1.3 km) north from this junction, you will find a parking area on the right. This is as far as vehicles should travel on this road.

From the parking area (0.0 mi.) the trail continues across the bridge over Cold Stream to private land. The route leaves the road and enters the woods. Following blue trail markers on a tote road through hardwood forest, you reach a cable barrier at 0.1 mi. (0.2 km). At 1.0 mi. (1.6 km) this flat route passes over a brook. Heading north, you cross a second brook at 2.0 mi. (3.9 km), after which rises and small pitches take you overland to a third brook at 2.4 mi. (3.9 km).

Swinging northwestward, a moderately steep slope soon begins. After gaining 180 ft. (55 m) in elevation, the trail again levels off, crosses several small brooks, and maintains its elevation at about 2000 ft. (612 m).

Descending slightly, you observe a PBM 1962 ft. (600 m) some 140 yds. (128 m) before the Fall Stream crossing. A small bridge takes you over Fall Stream, where a nice informal campsite is located. You may find bits and pieces of a heavy-gauge aluminum food storage container, strewn about and left by a bear many years ago. Fall Stream is at the 4.4 mi. (7.1 km) point and makes a good place for a rest break before the real exercise begins.

After following the left bank of the stream for about 150 yds. (138 m), the trail curves westward from the stream and begins a steady climb up a moderate grade. It levels off at 5.5 mi. (8.9 km). Now heading northwest, you descend an easy grade to a clearing at 5.9 mi. (9.6 km).

Crossing a small brook in the clearing, the trail passes a private camp that is on the right. Steady but gradual climbing takes you to the end of the clearing at 6.2 mi. (10.0 km). Soon after, the trail drops at a moderately steep rate and crosses the end of a vlei. From here you can see the remains of an old lumber camp, sitting on a hillside at the opposite side of the vlei. If time is not pressing, this might be an interesting side trip. As you continue your steady descent, you will see a side road to the right that leads generally in its direction.

At 6.8 mi. (11.0 km) the Jessup River is crossed on stones. In wet weather, a pair of logs at a campsite a few meters downstream provides a high water crossing. This region is frequently lumbered, and you may see evidence of current work.

Swinging to the right and again heading north, you follow an old lumber road. Part way up a moderate grade, the route makes a left turn off the road at 7.0 mi. (11.3 km) and, pitching sharply up a steep little slope, soon rejoins the lumber road.

Still climbing, you approach a major logging road near top of grade. The N-P trail swings left just before reaching it onto another tote road at 7.1 mi. (11.5 km). You continue the gradual climb for a while before the route finally levels. The trail enters another tote road as a trailing switch on the right at 7.5 mi. (12.2 km). A sign points the correct way.

You enter another lumbered area at 7.6 mi. (12.3 km) and cross Bloodgood Brook at 7.8 mi. (12.6 km). The trail now gradually climbs along a grassy lumber road and becomes moderately steep for a brief span before leveling. An abandoned camp on the left is passed at 8.8 mi. (14.3 km). You soon reach a brook, and cross a second brook on a bridge 125 yds. (115 m) before the trail junction to the first Spruce Lake lean-to at the outlet of the lake. At 9.4 mi. (15.2 km) a side trail to the left leads 0.2 mi. (0.3 km) to the lean-to. Set before a small sandy pair of beaches, it is not uncommon to watch feeding deer across the lake from this spot in the early morning light. However, being the closest lean-to to Piseco, it is also the most frequently used.

The trail continues along the east shore of Spruce Lake to a second trail junction at 10.1 mi. (16.4 km). Here, a side trail to the left leads down a moderate slope to another lean-to, tucked into a tiny clearing. Though this is not as pleasant a lean-to as the first, the swimming is excellent here.

Further along the shoreline, the N-P trail crosses the wide, rocky outlet of Balsam Lake. Thirty-five yds. (32 m) beyond, a third trail junction is reached, and a path to the left takes you to the third and most attractive of the Spruce Lake lean-tos. Set back in the trees a short distance, this is the oldest of the three, but since it is furthest along the trail it is the least used. It was built by members of the Adirondack Mountain Club. Just before reaching the lean-to, you pass a grassy clearing with an old refuse pile of articles brought in and left by sportsmen who were obviously too laden down on their return trip with big game to find room in the airplane for them.

Spruce Lake is a beautiful place. Loons still call in the night with piercing screams that bring you out of a sound sleep into instant alertness. Otter families can be seen playing in the water and cruising up and down the lake. It is a hard place to leave, unless you are heading further into this wilderness area.

Sucker Brook Trail

Difficulty: Moderately challenging
Round Trip Distance: 13.8 mi. (22.4 km)
Time Necessary: 2 days
Map: Indian Lake 15′ Series

The Sucker Brook Trail exemplifies a type of backpacking opportunity in the Adirondacks that is all too often overlooked. Most hikers want to climb a mountain or camp on the shore of a distant lake. Consequently, on reaching their destination they almost always meet others who had the same idea. Yet, on almost any map quadrangle of the Adirondacks, one can find trails that seem to head off into nowhere. Many a backpacker has spent countless hours of pleasure poring over maps and planning trips to such places. Finding good fishing spots, old mines, abandoned lumber camps, or even old survey points may be the ostensible reasons for such outings. When it comes right down to the nub of the matter, however, it's just plain fun to head into an area where the route isn't four feet wide with a bridge over every tiny brook. It is more challenging when you have to figure out for yourself how to get past a beaver bog or across a stream, and not knowing exactly where you will set up camp at night adds a little excitement to the trip.

Once you get used to the idea of seeking out-of-the-way locations, you'll find there's a great deal of space in the Adirondacks where you can be alone.

Eventually, bushwhacking trips may be your style. Real skill and woods savvy are needed for such experiences, but there's a certain sense of wilderness that can only be achieved by going it on your own.

The first part of the Sucker Brook Trail is well used by day hikers from Lewey Lake Public Campsite, and you follow a well maintained trail as far as the col between Cellar and Lewey Mountains. From the col, though, the route is a wilderness path where one can feel a real sense of isolation. As you head into the West Canada Lakes Wilderness Area, you will need to be resourceful to reach your goal. That's what makes it so enjoyable.

Access to the trailhead is on the north side of the bridge over the outlet of Lewey Lake. This is on Rte. 30 between Indian Lake and Speculator. Here, a macadam road leads west into tenting areas of the campsite. While it is possible to leave your vehicle at the roadside, it would be safer to leave it at the boat launching site nearby or at the campsite parking area, which is approximately 0.2 mi. (0.3 km) south of the bridge.

From Rte. 30, walk a short distance along the macadam road to a small clearing on the right. Here a sign (0.0 mi.) marks the official beginning of the trail. It is possible to remain on the macadam road, bearing right at a fork, to its end. You then hike up a grade past a gate to the right, where the trail is intersected.

The trail heads westward through hardwood forest. Gradually you realize that you are gaining elevation .The way is quite enjoyable. Occasionally, Sucker Brook is heard below you to the left, but it is seldom seen.

A large tributary stream is crossed at 1.3 mi. (2.1 km), and a steady grade takes you upward to the 2.3 mi. (3.7 km) point, where the trail levels and you follow the contour of the land for awhile.

Then, at 2.7 mi. (4.4 km), the trail markedly steepens. The next 0.3 mi. (0.5 km) is a steep climb to the col between Cellar and Lewey Mountains. From the col it is a relatively easy bushwhack to the summit of Lewey Mountain. Cellar Mountain's summit is a much stiffer climb through considerable blowdown.

The col is pleasantly level, with ferns and a white pine grove as a change of scenery. As the trail starts the descent towards Colvin Brook, it is readily apparent that fewer people travel this section. Well marked, the route narrows considerably. At times, when underbrush obscures the trail, only the markers can be seen ahead of you. This is a true wilderness trail, and a sense of the wild presses in on you as you go along.

At 4.6 mi. (7.5 km) Colvin Brook is reached; you will cross and recross this stream ten times before you leave it. Take care, since the rocks are slippery. In springtime it can be hazardous. You weave your way along the stream for about an hour, keeping a sharp eye out for trail markers.

Finally you veer from the stream for awhile, only to return at a point where beavers have taken advantage of a flat area to do extensive construction. After avoiding wet feet for a brief distance, you may find there is no alternative to wading across one section at 6.3 mi. (10.2 km). Bear to the left and use the alders for support. With diligence, you will quickly be back onto dry ground.

Donning dry footwear again, you proceed along the trail quite easily for the remaining distance to the lean-to. It is reached at 6.9 mi. (11.2 km) where it sits in a picturesque spot along the Cedar River.

Getting through a Wet Spot

The Cedar River is broad and shallow here. The crossing is slightly downstream from the lean-to and can be a bit tricky. If you plan to cross, plan your sequence of rock hops well or you may take a dunking.

The Sucker Brook Trail continues another 1.0 mi. (1.6 km) on a level course to a trail junction with the Northville-Placid Trail. This is just east of Lamphere Ridge.

Take your time on this trip, because it has a few spots where rushing can result in problems. But if you want the flavor of real wilderness, it is a fine outing.

Black River Wild Forest

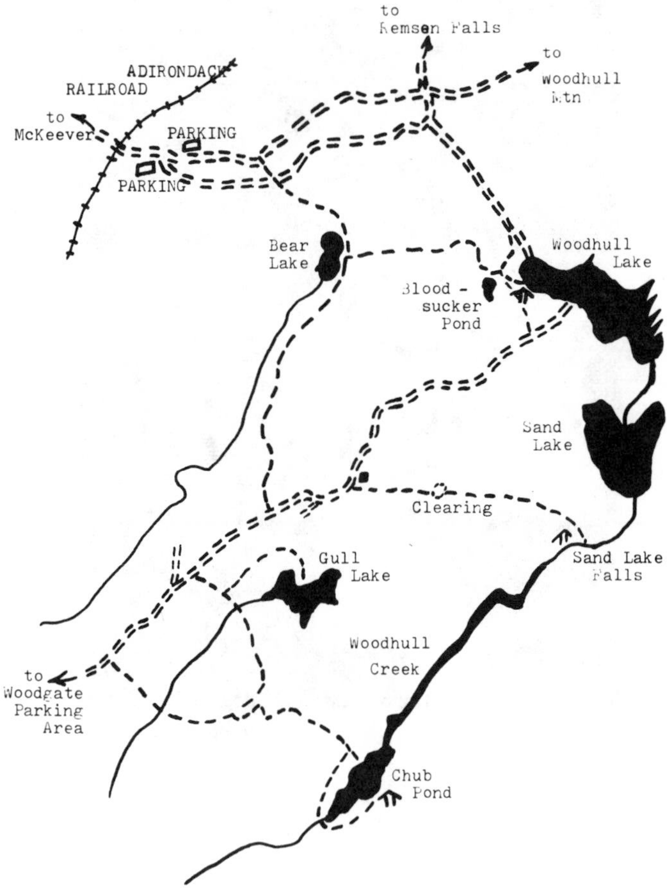

to Remsen Falls

to Woodhull Mtn

ADIRONDACK
RAILROAD

to McKeever

PARKING

PARKING

Bear Lake

Blood-sucker Pond

Woodhull Lake

Sand Lake

Clearing

Sand Lake Falls

Gull Lake

Woodhull Creek

to Woodgate Parking Area

Chub Pond

6. The Black River Wild Forest Area

The late 1700s saw Nat Foster and Jonathan "Jock" Wright running their traplines through these woods, just as Roscoe and Bert Conkling would do in later years. Lumbermen came as early as 1866, when Phil McGuire of Punkeytown (Forestport) cut down trees to provide spars for Yankee and British shipbuilders. Rev. A. L. Byron-Curtiss led an influx of "city sports" to this area when he began summering at North Lake in 1892.

Canal builders started pressing for a "forest preserve" when the headwaters of the Black River and its canal began to close off due to the flooding effects of the then current lumbering practices. Some people, seeing what was coming, bought up huge acreage for private clubs before the state could create the Forest Preserve. The Adirondack League Club, Lookout Mountain Club, and the Bisby Club were a few of the major organizations to form in this region.

The Forest Preserve was created, but lumbering still continued on private lands well into the 20th century. The last great logging river run in the Adirondacks occurred on the Moose River when the McKeever crib dam broke on June 3, 1947, sending thousands of logs downriver. You can still see the remains of the dam as you cross the Rte. 28 bridge over the Moose River at McKeever.

Today, this area has thirty miles of trails and thirty-six bodies of water. The winter brings a few trappers and many snowmobilers into this country, but in summer only a few fishermen and hikers get off the beaten paths. Chub, Gull, Woodhull, Sand, and Nicks lakes are but a few of the places backpackers can go for interesting outings.

Big Woodhull Lake and Bear Lake Loop

Difficulty: Easy, with a few moderate grades.
Round Trip Distance: 9.3 mi. (15.1 km)
Time Necessary: 2 days
Map: McKeever 15' Series

Topographic maps refer to it as Woodhull Lake, but DEC trail signs call it Big Woodhull to prevent its being confused with Little Woodhull Lake a few miles to the south. The hiker will find a variety of trail types on this outing. The first part of the hike follows the old road to Woodhull Lake. The state made it into a fire truck road, so it is quite good as far as the Remsen Falls junction. From there on, it is an unimproved snowmobile trail. In contrast, the return trip via Bear Lake is a marvelous woods trail of quite recent construction. Bear Lake, unless affected by beaver activity, is completely surrounded by sandy beach.

Access to the trailhead is off Rte. 28 at McKeever. The turnoff is to the east, a little over a mile north of Otter Lake Village. A state road sign indicates the hamlet of McKeever on the south side of Moose River. Drive along the old macadam road 0.2 mi. (0.3 km) from Rte. 28. At a curve in the road bear right onto a gravel road, pass the old railroad station, and cross the railroad tracks a short distance further along the way. Proceed along a level dirt road 0.4 mi. (0.6 km) to a large DEC snowmobile parking area. The snowmobile trail forks to the right but you should continue driving on the left fork past the parking area. Another 0.1 mi. (0.2 km) of driving will bring you to a second parking area and DEC trail register for the hiking route.

DAY 1

The truck trail heads east from the gate (0.0 mi.) at the end of the parking area. Rarely seen red trail markers guide you along an almost flat sandy trail. Closed to vehicles except in emergency, this trail makes a nice cross-country ski trail in the winter. The lane in summer is grassy and the walk enjoyably easy.

At 0.9 mi. (1.5 km), a DEC trail sign indicates that a side trail to the right follows blue trail markers to Bear Lake. Continue straight ahead on the truck road. Ferns and moss covered boulders are numerous. Three clearings are passed. Two have brooks running through them. Willows and black spruces surround the openings in the forest.

A four-way trail junction is reached at 2.8 mi. (4.5 km), about an hour after you begin the hike. To the left, the trail leads 0.7 mi. (1.2 km) to the Moose River and the Remsen Falls lean-to on the far shore. The trail straight ahead leads another 3.2 mi. (5.2 km) to a side trail which extends 2.5 mi. (4.1 km) up to the summit of Woodhull Mountain.

Turn right and follow blue trail markers up a moderate grade. This section of road is less used and more narrow. At 3.0 mi. (4.9 km), an extended wire cable crosses the road and weaves through the woods on each side for several meters. Thirty yards (28 m) beyond, the snowmobile trail from McKeever enters from the right front.

Turn left at this acute junction and head down a curving grade along the snowmobile route. A difference between wild forest and wilderness designated Forest Preserve land is immediately obvious. In the wilderness no vehicular traffic is permitted. On some wild forest roads, however, where there has been a historic record of vehicular use before land designation was assigned, vehicles are still permitted. Apparently, such is the case here. Hunters have used vehicles, and in steep areas their tires have gouged out ruts. Fortunately, though, there aren't too many of these spots in the stretch of trail you have to hike.

The grade ranges from gradual to moderate. In the next 1.3 mi. (2.1 km) 340 ft. (104 m) elevation will be gained. The trail levels periodically, and in one of these level zones, on the right at approximately 4.0 mi. (6.5 km), there is a large hunters' campsite. Height of land is reached at 4.3 mi. (7.0 km). An unmarked trail junction is located here. The road straight ahead leads 0.2 mi. (0.3 km) down to Wolf Landing on Big Woodhull Lake.

Turn right at this junction. As you begin a swing around the west shore of Big Woodhull Lake, elevation is gradually lost. You can catch glimpses of the lake to the left. The trail is quite nice.

The woods trail from Bear Lake enters from the right at 4.6 mi. (7.5 km). A few meters further on you cross the outlet of Bloodsucker Brook. Immediately there is another trail junction. The right fork, with blue markers, is the snowmobile trail to Sand Lake and Woodgate. Turn left here and follow red trail markers along a woods path. Big Woodhull Lake and its lean-to are reached at 4.8 mi. (7.8 km).

This large body of water has rock along much of its shoreline and is most appealing. If the lean-to is not the largest in the Adirondack Park, it must run a close second. This incredible structure has a double fireplace and will easily hold twenty people. Unfortunately, numerous trees have been cut down around it.

DAY 2

From the lean-to (0.0 mi.), return 0.2 mi. (0.3 km) to the Bear Lake trail junction beside Bloodsucker Brook.

Turn left and follow yellow trail markers up the left side of Bloodsucker Brook. At 0.3 mi. (0.5 km) a well built beaver dam is passed, and soon thereafter Bloodsucker Pond appears to the left front. In spite of its name this is a most attractive sheet of water. Blueberry bushes form a necklace around this hidden jewel in the forest, and beaver meadows surround it.

The path heads to the north across rolling terrain. It is a comparatively new trail and is very comfortable to walk on. The fern covered forest floor is lush. After about ten minutes of walking, the path swings to the west and begins the long, effortless, gradual decline to Bear Lake. Gentle grades and a soft trail make hiking this stretch a pleasure.

A large inlet of Bear Lake is approached at 1.6 mi. (2.6 km). This is followed to the lake. After ten minutes of walking you find yourself high above the stream; then you rapidly drop downward as you reach Bear Lake at 2.0 mi. (3.2 km).

Several good but informal campsites are found where the inlet enters the lake. A blue marked DEC trail intersects from the right and continues southward to the Bear Creek parking area at Woodgate. The lake sits in a basin, surrounded by a high horseshoe-shaped ridge on its northern end. The southern end opens up, and from its outlet Bear Creek drains through miles of wetlands. The shore is entirely lined by a fine gravel and sand beach which invites swimming. The presence of such an alluring lake here is somehow unexpected, and one is tempted to stay here and camp. Certainly, one could have an interesting weekend on this shore.

You cross the inlet and follow the blue marked trail around the eastern shoreline, heading northward. Fifty yards (46 m) after crossing another inlet at the north end of the lake on a log bridge, the trail makes an abrupt turn to the right. From here it mounts a moderate grade, winding up through a narrow gorge. At 2.4 mi. (3.9 km), water pirouettes off a high cliff, gliding downward to join the brook you have been following. Soon after, height of land is reached and you proceed on level ground for a few minutes. You then begin a long gradual descent to the McKeever truck trail.

A stream is crossed several times. At 3.2 mi. (5.2 km) a short side trail to the left leads to a small shelter under a large boulder, just off the trail. From this point you descend a brief moderate grade and negotiate a flat wet section. The muddy, rutted, snowmobile trail is crossed at 3.4 mi. (5.8 km). Continue to follow along the left side of the brook. The truck trail is reached at 3.6 mi. (5.8 km).

Turn left and return 0.9 mi. (1.5 km) to the McKeever parking area. This is reached at 4.5 mi. (7.3 km).

Sand Lake Falls

Difficulty: Easy, but watch where you're going.
Round Trip Distance: 11.8 mi. (19.1 km)
Time Necessary: 2 days
Map: McKeever 15' Series

This trip takes you to an isolated lean-to by a broad waterfall having dozens of deep cold water trout holes in the cascades below it. Not far away, a wide stillwater extends for a great distance through protected forest. A network of old logging roads is followed: some are still used by vehicles, others are grassy lanes, and some need brushing out (1980). Trail markers are well posted where needed and absent when the way is obvious. However, the backpacker will have to be alert to changes in direction at numerous intersections.

Access to the trailhead is off Rte. 28 at Woodgate. Turn east onto Bear Creek Road at the blinker light. Proceed along this road as far as you can travel. The railroad tracks are passed at 2.2 mi. (3.6 km), and you reach the DEC Bear Creek parking area and trail register at 3.2 mi. (5.2 km).

The trail begins at the end of the parking area and follows blue trail markers along the old Woodhull Lake road, which is now a snowmobile trail. A brief grade soon levels out. At 0.2 mi. (0.3 km), DEC trail signs are posted at a road junction. Continue straight ahead to a second fork in the road at 0.3 mi. (0.5 km). The fork to the right is a muddy route leading to Gull Lake and Chub Pond and, according to a posted sign, requires winches on vehicles. The left fork has a cable barrier.

Turn left at the fork and follow trail markers which are now yellow in color. A grassy lane takes you through a mixed wood forest. Frequent branch trails are passed on both sides of the road. After about fifteen minutes of walking, at 0.9 mi. (1.5 km), still another trail junction is reached. The grassy road forks to the left, but your trail forks right. It would be easy to miss this particular change in direction if you were not watching for trail markers.

Occasional vehicle ruts are seen, but the road is generally an enjoyable route. A trail junction at 1.5 mi. (2.4 km) occurs when a branch road to Gull Lake and Chub Pond heads to the right. For hikers this would be the preferred route to those bodies of water. Gull Lake lean-to is approximately 1.5 mi. (2.4 km). Chub Pond is approximately 3.4 mi. (5.5 km), but its lean-to is on the opposite side of the lake, 5.1 mi. (8.3 km) from this junction.

Continue straight ahead. A multitude of ferns lines the trail. The route makes a broad swing to the right at 2.5 mi. (4.1 km). Here the Bear Lake trail is indicated by a signpost on the outside of the curve. That trail leads past Coleman Dam approximately 3.0 mi. (4.9 km) on a blue marked route to Bear Lake.

For a short distance the road heads southeast, reaching a T-junction at 2.6 mi. (4.2 km). Here, signs direct you to turn left.

Another five minutes of walking brings you to the first good drinking water, a small stream flowing through a culvert. You then begin a long gradual upgrade over a minor ridge, with a similar gradual downgrade on its opposite side.

At 3.2 mi. (5.2 km) a major trail junction is reached, within sight of a large building 250 ft. (76 m) to your front. The yellow marked trail forks left and continues approximately 3.7 mi. (6.0 km) to the lean-to at Woodhull Lake. The trail right leads 2.7 mi. (4.4 km) to Sand Lake Falls.

The remaining portion of the trip passes along a snowmobile route that doesn't appear to have been used for several years (1980). In a few places the undergrowth is closing in on the sides of the trail, but trail markers are very well posted and the majority of the route is easily followed. The worst part is the first 200 yds (183 km) from this junction.

Turn right and follow blue trail markers from the trail signs. Yellow snowmobile markers are also posted along the way. The trail passes through a short zone of blowdown and heavy undergrowth; you are in a small gully and the correct way follows it, curving to the right in a gradual arc. You soon cross a hunter's trail. Avoid it, and avoid a second hunter's trail that enters from the left a shorter distance along the way. A small opening with branching logging roads is soon reached. A trail sign points to the correct route, which crosses a branch of Mill Creek on a wooden bridge. Bearing left, the route becomes quite easy to follow.

You walk generally eastward with little change in grade and reach a large clearing at 4.0 mi. (6.5 km). Apple trees and various pieces of old implements give evidence that someone once called this place home. Nature is reclaiming it as small spruce invade, but it still is an interesting place to poke around and to try to imagine who may have lived here more than fifty years ago.

The route sidles along the right side of the clearing and returns to the woods at the east corner of the old homestead. A wet stretch is passed before a gradual increase in elevation begins. The route is generally east. Gentle grades continue to 5.6 mi. (9.1 km), where direction of travel becomes increasingly to the southeast. A descent begins. Several small brooks are crossed as you drop down into the Woodhull Creek valley.

A junction for a trail is reached at 5.7 mi. (9.2 km); you may miss it on the way in, but it can easily be taken on the way out. Blue arrows are painted on a beech tree. (This trail turns left and heads generally northeast in the direction of the trail from Sand Lake to North Lake, which it probably joins. It has no DEC markers but follows tree blazes which are painted blue. A hunter's camp and well constructed garbage pit are a short distance along this trail. The trail itself is much better maintained than the DEC trail you are following.) Remember to bear left at this junction on the return trip and head northwest.

You continue to descend the open trail. The sounds of rushing water are heard long before the charging stream comes into sight. The first indication of the lean-to is when its glittering wood shingle roof catches your eye. The trail swings around to the front of the lean-to and enters a very large clearing where a small but excellent lean-to faces Woodhull Creek.

Sand Lake Falls

The lean-to sits well back from the top of Sand Lake Falls. Perhaps 35 yds. (32 m) of clearing separate the shelter from the wide stream. Sand Lake Falls is wide, but not especially high. It tumbles from one deep pool to another for hundreds of meters downstream as it slices its way through Adirondack bedrock.

One finds it hard to imagine what this great rushing stream is doing here until several maps are studied. Big Woodhull Lake drains into Sand Lake. Sand Lake and all four lakes of the Bisby Chain drain into Woodhull Creek. Consequently, the waters of six lakes plunge over Sand Lake Falls. Temporarily held in a stillwater over a kilometer long above the falls, the water shoots into the wide gorge. Gravity pulls it ever onward to Chub Pond, Kayuta Lake at Forestport, and finally to the Black River. Such a spectacle in this isolated forest is like an oasis in the desert.

The snowmobile trail heads out of the far side of the clearing. It parallels the stream but is not in sight of it. The great, wide stillwater is 0.2 mi. (0.3 km) beyond the lean-to and should be visited. Though the snowmobile trail ends at the shore of the stillwater, deer trails provide easy routes along its edge for quite a distance. All manner of waterfowl can be seen on this protected waterway, where the deer seem genuinely surprised to see a human.

7. The Ha-De-Ron-Dah Wilderness Area

The Ha-de-ron-dah Wilderness Area is a 26,600 acre forest on the west side of Rte. 28, generally south and west of Old Forge. In this section of the Adirondacks, one usually thinks of the three branches of the Moose River. Though the outflow of the fifty-nine bodies of water of the Ha-de-ron-dah eventually joins the Moose River near Lyonsdale, a separate watershed actually exists. All of the lakes and ponds mentioned in this section drain generally westward into Pine Creek and then on to the Moose and Black Rivers.

Within the area's forest is a considerable variety of floral associations. The southern half has had significant fire damage in the past, which was severe enough to affect the soils. As the earth rebuilds its fertility, numerous bracken fern, berry bushes, pin cherry, and aspen are seen. North of the Big Otter Lake truck trail, on the other hand, pines up to forty inches in diameter can be found. In between, a hardwood forest of yellow birch, beech, and maple grows. Low areas have wetlands and beaver meadows.

Less than a 1000 ft. (306 m) change in elevation is found in this region, and no more than a 250 ft. (76 m) change is found on the trails described here. In general, long easy routes with occasional short ups and downs typify this rolling terrain.

The Civilian Conservation Corps (CCC) built the Big Otter Lake truck trail in the 1930s to permit quicker reaction to any future forest fires. It's still usable for that purpose today, but it is becoming a grassy lane where walking is most enjoyable. The large old stone fireplace just before the gate at Thendara is all that is left of the CCC camp that once occupied the open meadow here. A snowmobile club is planning to incorporate the fireplace into part of a building addition they are making to their clubhouse (1980). It is fitting that fires should once again burn in this historic structure.

The six lean-tos of this region and many of the 27.3 mi. (44.2 km) of foot trails are seldom used. Few people seem to know the area well. Those who do tend to come back to it year after year. It is good hiking country.

Middle Branch Lake via the Big Otter Lake Truck Trail

Difficulty: Easy and relaxing.
Round Trip Distance: 11.8 mi. (19.1 km)
Time Necessary: 2 days
Map: McKeever 15' Series

This outing takes you over very gentle trails to a nice little lake. It is one of the better beginner hikes because there are no major grades. The larger portion of the trip is along the Big Otter Lake truck trail. This old road is slowly growing in and is quite pleasant to travel. The last mile to the lean-to is a true woods trail and makes a nice variation. By using the Cedar Pond crossover trail, both hikes described here can be combined to make a much longer outing possible.

Ha-De-Ron-Dah Wilderness Area

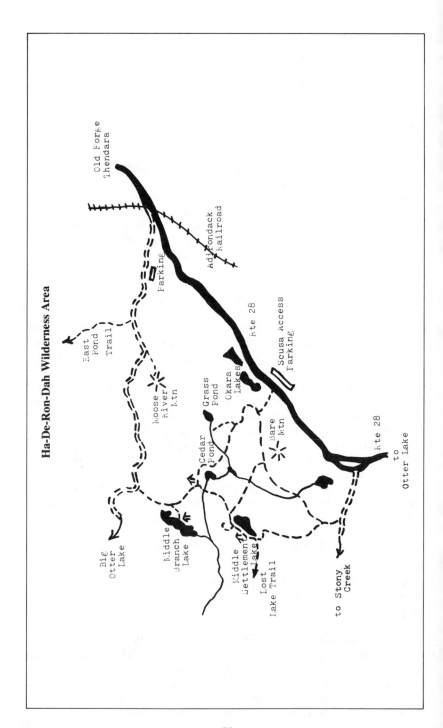

Access to the trailhead is off Rte. 28, south of Old Forge and Thendara. Immediately south of the railroad underpass at Thendara a gravel road turns west. There is no sign, but the road leads 0.4 mi. (0.6 km) to a parking area and road barrier. In the winter, both a snowmobile trail and the excellent cross country ski trail along the Big Otter Lake truck trail originate at this point. (They soon split.) In the summer, only an early morning deer is seen here.

From the DEC register and road barrier (0.0 mi.), the route follows blue trail markers up a short moderate grade. At 0.1 mi. (0.2 km) the snowmobile trail splits to the right and the hiking trail continues along the road. Another, more effective, vehicle barrier is seen at 0.4 mi. (0.6 km). A short moderate grade past the barrier soon becomes a long gradual stroll downward before it levels off near Indian Brook. Glimpses of beaver houses are seen across the meadows through the trees. A flat, wide sandy stretch takes you across the Indian Brook flood plain at 1.0 mi. (1.6 km). Insects and birds of every description are found here.

The trail gains slight elevation and the way becomes wooded again as you come off the flood plain. At 1.5 mi. (2.4 km) a trail junction is reached where the East Pond trail branches to the right. Tents are needed for camping at East Pond since the lean-to burned down.

The road from the junction begins a steady incline, making the Moose River Mountain trail junction seem further than it really is from the East Pond trail junction. This junction is located near height of land at the 2.2 mi. (3.6 km) point; a widening of the trail and a Big Otter Lake distance sign mark the spot. The fire tower has been removed from the mountain, but the unmarked trail to the left looks well used (1980). It leads another mile, and 200 ft. (61 m) of elevation are gained before the summit is reached.

From height of land the truck trail begins a stepped, easy decline of gradual grades. Occasional large beeches are seen. As they age, a fungus attacks them from within their cores, and they eventually become victims of strong winds and topple over. Examine the hollowed centers of these giants.

A major tributary running off Moose River Mountain crosses the trail in a spruce lowland at 3.7 mi. (6.0 km) on its way to the South Inlet of Big Otter Lake. An informal campsite is on the right of the trail. This is a good place for a rest.

Continuing on easy trail, another short moderate decline brings you to the Middle Branch Lake trail junction at 4.9 mi. (7.9 km). A sign indicates you should turn left and follow yellow trail markers. The route from here to the lake is over a forest path where footing must be closely watched. The change in trail type is welcome, however. The course is generally to the south through a young forest of smaller trees.

Another junction is found at 5.6 mi. (9.1 km). Here, the crossover trail to Cedar Pond forks to the left. It is 0.9 mi. (1.5 km) of moderately tough trail over two ridges.

Middle Branch Lake is straight ahead on a red marked trail. The vegetation again changes as you pass through an old burn area. Many bracken fern and a more open woods greet you. You pass a large pyramidal boulder just before you reach the lean-to at 5.9 mi. (9.6 km).

The lean-to sits above the water on a small point overlooking the lake. Your view from the midpoint of the eastern shoreline is to the southwest. This attractive body of water has a pair of sedate loons (1980). A few informal campsites are near the lean-to, and fishermen have made paths along the shore of the lake.

Middle Settlement Lake via the Scusa Access Trail

Difficulty: Easy to moderate
Round Trip Distance: 7.8 mi. (12.6 km)
Time Necessary: 2 days
Map: McKeever 15' Series

This loop route leads to what many feel is the nicest lean-to in the Ha-de-ron-dah Wilderness Area. It certainly has an attractive setting. Unfortunately, the trails leading to it are not as interesting as those in the more northern sections.

At the lake there is an interesting cave to see, a lookout ledge to climb, and a large beaver dam to observe. This lean-to is frequently used by snowshoers for winter camping.

Access to the trailhead is from a large parking area with picnic tables just south of the Okara Lakes. This is on the southeast side of Rte. 28 approximately 2.9 mi. (4.7 km) south of the railroad underpass at Thendara, near Old Forge. The trailhead begins on private land across the road from the north end of this parking area. A sign indicates the way to state land.

DAY 1

The trail leading to state land is called the Scusa Access Trail. From Rte. 28 (0.0 mi.) cross the wooden bridge over the small outlet of the Okara Lakes to where a DEC trail register and trail signs are located. Follow red trail markers.

The hardest part of the trip now leads up a moderately steep slope 0.1 mi. (0.2 km) to a bare rock opening. Imbedded in this rocky ridge are both milky and rose quartz. The trail then gradually loses elevation, crossing two small brooks on log walks before regaining some of the lost elevation.

The trail junction with the Brown Tract Trail is reached at 0.6 mi. (1.0 km). Middle Settlement Lake can be reached by traveling in either direction from this junction, but the lay of the land is such that a counterclockwise loop is preferable. It is therefore recommended that you turn to the right (northeastward).

Turning right, follow both yellow and red trail markers. Avoid the unmarked trail you will soon see to your right. Approximately 100 ft. (31 m) further on, at 0.8 mi. (1.3 km), another junction is reached.

Your trail turns sharply left here and continues to follow red markers. The Brown Tract Trail continues straight ahead 2.5 mi. (4.1 km) to the Okara Lakes parking area.

A few minutes along the Cedar Pond trail a wet area is crossed on an unusually long log walk. Immediately thereafter a junction is reached, just before a moderate grade begins. A few meters to the right are some trail signs, and the uphill trail from those signs soon merges with the red marked trail you have been following. The grade levels and then continues over rolling terrain. Some ten minutes later a moderate grade takes you down to a small brook. On the opposite side of the

Middle Settlement Lake

brook at 1.1 mi. (1.8 km) is another trail junction. The yellow marked trail to the right leads 0.5 mi. (0.8 km) north to a campsite beside Grass Pond.

Bear left and continue to follow red trail markers. You walk on the level for awhile before beginning a gradual decline to the crossing of the Grass Pond outlet at 1.7 mi. (2.8 km). This large rushing stream is a good place to get a drink and rest. If you look downstream, you can see the beginning of an unnamed pond from which this outflow of Grass Pond continues on to Cedar Pond.

Beyond the outlet, you climb a few meters away from the water to drier ground. Then, heading downstream, you parallel the stream. Generally keeping to the contour, you drop into occasional dips as small brooks are crossed. You begin a gradual descent at 2.3 mi. (3.7 km) and can see Cedar Pond through the trees to your left front. The trail swings along the north side of Cedar Pond but is well back from the shoreline.

Fifteen minutes later two small, shallow, clear flowing creeks are crossed. The far bank of the second one is steep. The Cedar Pond lean-to is another five minutes ahead of you. The trail follows a hummock ridge through spruce and passes a spring 45 yds. (41 m) before reaching the lean-to at 3.0 mi. (4.9 km).

The lean-to is not in good shape. The roof leaks (1980) and half of the floor is missing. However, very credible tenting sites could be established. Cedar Pond is about 0.2 mi. (0.3 km) away and can be reached by a little used trail that proceeds straight ahead from the clearing, opposite the front of the lean-to.

Most hikers won't be impressed with the marshy wetlands of the almost filled in north end of Cedar Pond. Its water is murky when you can find it. Botanists, however, may wish to spend a whole weekend here because of the great variety of water plants available for study. Black spruces form a nice background setting, and there are abundant blueberry bushes on the marshland. It is an interesting ecosystem.

At the left rear of the lean-to is the junction of three trails. The crossover trail to Middle BranchLake heads to the right in a generally northward direction and follows yellow trail markers 1.2 mi. (1.9 km) over a pair of moderately steep ridges to the lean-to on Middle Branch Lake. The trail you should follow is the Middle Settlement Lake trail to the left, which also follows yellow trail markers but heads to the south.

The trail is a soft woods path. Some elevation is gained and the wetlands of Cedar Pond can be seen in the distance to your left. At 3.4 mi. (5.5 km), the trail makes an abrupt left hand turn, drops down, and crosses the outlet of Cedar Pond on a log bridge. A swampy area is crossed with little difficulty before minor elevation is gained and you reach drier ground. To the right the ground begins to rise sharply, and finally you reach rock cliffs with boulders at their base.

An immense boulder is passed on the left at 4.0 mi. (6.5 km). Just past it, on the right, is a smaller boulder, which has a small cave under it. Rocks have been used to fill in open spots around its entrance. At one time a wooden bed was inside, and winter campers have been known to sleep there.

A small creek is crossed 70 yds. (64 m) beyond the huge boulder. The Middle Settlement Lake Access Trail junction comes in from the left, on the far side of the creek. Turning right, you reach the shallow silted end of Middle Settlement Lake after traveling a few more meters.

The trail bears right, along the north shore of the lake. It soon comes very close to the shore at a grassy spot. Immediately afterward, a junction is reached. A large sign is located here, but the whole junction can be missed if you are gazing out at the lake, which has become increasingly more attractive. This red markered side trail leads 0.2 mi. (0.3 km) to a rocky ledge some 150 ft. (46 m) above the lake surface. From the ledge you can get a fairly good view of the surrounding country. You may wish to make the climb after depositing your pack at the lean-to.

As the trail moves a little further back from the shore, you pass an informal campsite before reaching the lean-to at 4.5 mi. (7.3 km).

The lean-to is about two-thirds of the way down the lake and sits about 10 ft. (3 m) above the water on a large rock outcrop. The view is marvelous, and the changes in light intensity on the far shore as the sun drops behind you at sunset are a delight to behold. Deep water beyond the rock outcrop invites you to a refreshing swim.

There are two informal campsites further along the trail past the lean-to. You should walk down the trail to the lake outlet, where there is a wide beaver dam over 6 ft. (2 m) high.

DAY 2

You could make a longer loop than the one described here by continuing southwestward on this trail beyond the lake outlet until it connects up with the Brown Tract Trail again. This would make the return trip 5.7 mi. (9.2 km) instead of the 3.3 mi. (5.3 km) trip described here. However, you should be prepared to wade through waist deep water when crossing Middle Settlement Creek.

The suggested return trip retraces the trail 0.5 mi. (0.8 km) back to the aforementioned trail junction with the Middle Settlement Lake Access Trail. The blue marked trail has mostly gradual grades with some minor ups and downs as streams are crossed. A small ridge and then two wet areas are crossed. Both have log walks. From the second one, at 1.4 mi. (2.3 km), you can see the same unnamed wetland pond to the left that you saw yesterday from the opposite side when you crossed the outlet of Grass Pond.

A gentle upgrade takes you through a section of raspberries and ferns to the trail junction with the Brown Tract Trail at 1.7 mi. (2.8 km).

Turn left here and follow yellow trail markers. The character of the forest rapidly changes to more mature hardwoods as you reach higher ground. The grades are so gradual that height of land is barely noticed at 2.2 mi. (3.6 km). A gradual, almost flat, trail takes you downward. Finally. after a last moderate drop to a stream crossing, you reach the Scusa Access Trail junction at 2.7 mi. (4.4 km).

Turn right and follow red trail markers 0.6 mi. (1.0 km) to Rte. 28, reached at 3.3 mi. (5.3 km).

For additional trips in this area and the following, refer to *Guide to Adirondack Trails: West-Central Region* by Art Haberl (ADK).

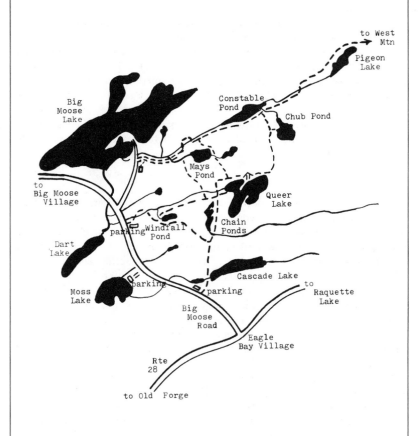

8. The Pigeon Lake Wilderness Area

The Pigeon Lake Wilderness Area extends from Stillwater Reservoir to Raquette Lake. Together with the Five Ponds Wilderness Area and the newly acquired (1979) Nehasane Area, an immense block of wilderness is found in which relatively few foot trails exist. Often it has been the backpacking skier, in the dead of winter, who has penetrated this land. A small network of trails does exist, however.

In 1876 Jim Higby built a rough bark shanty for William Dutton on the North Shore of Big Moose Lake, and in 1878 Jack Sheppard built a permanent camp for some New York sportsmen. Other camps appeared in the region, but the difficulty of access kept this country from ever becoming densely populated. Still, resorts were built. The sensational murder of Grace Brown by Chester Gillette on Big Moose Lake in 1906 drew temporary attention and was later chronicled by Theodore Dreiser in *An American Tragedy.*

Within the 50,800 acres of the Pigeon Lake Wilderness Area lie some sixty-four bodies of water. Only four lean-tos are found here and two of them must be reached by water. The backpacker will need a tent and be prepared to rough it, but the country is magnificent.

Fishermen and hunters have made many woods trails. There is opportunity for a true wilderness experience in this region, and those with the necessary knowledge and skills will find the kind of country few realize still exists in the Adirondacks.

The two outings described here may be linked to make a longer trip. It is also possible to continue northeast from Constable Pond to Pigeon Lake and West Mountain. The trip into West Mountain is rough, and you must be prepared to get your feet wet. But it can be a great trip for the experienced backpacker.

Queer Lake via the Chain Ponds Loop

Round Trip Distance: 8.6 mi. (13.9 km)
Difficulty: Easy to moderate
Time Necessary: 2 days
Map: Big Moose 15′ Series

Few outings give you the sense of wilderness as quickly as this one. Though reasonably close to a public highway, only a few fishermen and hunters head back into this country. The majority of them, however, head directly for Queer Lake from Windfall Pond; thus, the Chain Ponds Loop is still wild and primitive. The trail is a true woodspath, not a wide thoroughfare, but it is well marked and for the most part in excellent condition. The only lean-to is found at Queer Lake, but all of the ponds have informal campsites. It is as a backpacking trail should be.

Trailhead access is from the DEC parking area on the Eagle Bay–Big Moose Road. This is 3.3 mi. (5.3 km) from Eagle Bay and about 1.9 mi. (3.1 km) north of the Moss Lake parking area. The small sign on the north side of the road can easily be missed if you're not looking for it. The parking area is quite large but hidden by trees.

Trail distances given in this section are often at variance with the posted trail signs seen on the trails.

DAY 1

From the DEC register (0.0 mi.), follow the yellow marked trail east 0.2 mi. (0.3 km) to where it turns left and crosses a bridge. The trail straight ahead leads to an informal campsite.

You climb over two small knolls and at 0.7 mi. (1.1 km) recross the creek at a point where the water cascades through a small flume. The trail turns left and parallels the creek for a ways to Beaver Meadow, then bears right and climbs beside Windfall Pond outlet to a trail junction at 1.1 mi. (1.8 km) at Windfall Pond. The left fork trail leads 1.6 mi. (2.6 km) to Queer Lake's shore.

Turning right from this junction, follow the blue marked trail up a short moderate grade to the southeast. There is a nice view of Windfall Pond below to your left before you turn into the immense hardwood forest.

After ten minutes on a true woods path, you approach a small col having a rocky wall covered with thick mosses. A gradual descent takes you to the edge of a large pond at 1.5 mi. (2.4 km).

Swinging left of the pond, you gradually ascend again and see more interesting rock formations on your left. These rock structures have considerable quartz in them. Small caves, cracks, and moss growths attract your attention. The trail follows a narrow gully which presses in on you.

At 2.5 mi. (4.1 km) you reach the Cascade Lake Link Trail at a junction. The red marked trail to the right leads 2.0 mi. (3.2 km) to Cascade Lake.

Turn left here, still following the blue markers. Drop down and across the narrow gully floor you have been paralleling and cross it. Some ups and downs eventually become just downs, and you reach Chain Ponds at 2.9 mi. (4.7 km).

The trail crosses a brook which connects a vlei on your right to the most southern of the three Chain Ponds on the left. The clear waters and open woods make this an attractive location. The trail skirts the east shore after climbing a small incline. For several minutes you drink in the beauty of the pond as you walk along. Finally, you veer away from the water and make a brief climb to a defile through the ridge at 3.2 mi. (5.2 km). This narrow pass has rugged cliffs rising to your right, with all manner of small conifers clinging to its sides. One gets the feeling of primeval.

Once through the defile a long descent begins, ending at a four way trail junction at Queer Lake. This is reached at 3.8 mi. (6.2 km). A few meters to your right is Queer Lake. The Windfall Pond trail is to your left.

Straight ahead (northwest) is the trail you should follow to the lean-to. You cross the wet outlet of Queer Lake on a long log walk and follow the perimeter of

A Wilderness Trail—Pigeon Lake Area

the lake a short distance. The trail then makes an abrupt lefthand turn and climbs a moderate grade. Be sure you don't miss this turn and take the unmarked fishermen's path that continues along the lake shore.

Continue along your route to the Mays Pond trail junction at 4.2 mi. (6.8 km). Do not turn left onto the Mays Pond trail even though it has the same yellow trail markers you have been following since the last trail junction. Keep to the trail you have been on until a stand of hemlocks is reached at 4.5 mi. (7.3 km). Here, the yellow marked Chub Pond trail turns left. Avoid it.

Instead, bear right and follow the red marked trail down the grade to the lake shore. A log walk takes you across the soggy approach to the peninsula where the lean-to is situated. Follow the western edge of the peninsula to its narrow neck. Then cross over to the eastern side, where you'll quickly arrive at the lean-to at 4.8 mi. (7.8 km). Should you miss the crossover spot, you'll walk another five minutes before arriving at the end of the long peninsula.

Whoever built the Queer Lake lean-to knew how to do a proper job. Set in a grassy clearing, it catches breezes off the lake all day long. It has a good fireplace. Even the deacon's seat has a notch cut in it so you can easily sweep debris from the lean-to. An eaves trough keeps rain water from dripping in front of the lean-to.

Queer Lake is queer only in that its unusually large peninsula results in a very odd shaped lake. You'll probably want to trek to the end of the peninsula and go swimming.

DAY 2

From the lean-to (0.0 mi.), travel the 1.0 mi. (1.6 km) back to the Chain Ponds trail junction at the southern end of the lake. Turn right and head west for Windfall Pond. A level well used trail follows yellow markers through hardwoods. A log walk takes you across a wet area. Still on the level, you walk beside a stream until you reach a junction at 1.3 mi. (2.1 km). An unmarked trail continues straight ahead to the privately owned Hermitage camp. Your trail turns sharply left. Proceeding up a moderately steep grade, you soon descend back down to the valley floor. The Hermitage Trail junction is reached at 1.5 mi. (2.4 km). The red marked Hermitage Trail leads 1.3 mi. (2.1 km) northwest to the West Mountain Trail from Higby Road.

Continue straight ahead on a gradual descent for about ten minutes, then bear left up a moderate grade. Midway up the grade, the trail swings to the right, following the contour along the ridge. A large meadow can be seen down below to your right through the trees. Walking is easy and rate of travel is rapid from this point onward. It doesn't seem long until Windfall Pond is seen below you to the left, sitting in a sheltered basin. Circling down to it, you reach an informal campsite beside its outlet at 2.7 mi. (4.4 km). The Chain Pond Loop junction is just across the outlet.

From here, you return the 1.1 mi. (1.8 km) to Big Moose Road, previously described on Day 1. This is reached at 3.8 mi. (4.2 km).

Chub Pond—Mays Pond Loop

Round Trip Distance: 10.1 mi. (16.4 km)
Difficulty: Easy, Day 1; moderately difficult, Day 2
Time Necessary: 2 days
Map: Big Moose 15′ Series

On this outing the backpacker visits several pristine bodies of wilderness water. No lean-tos are available at the recommended camping spots, so a tent is essential. Small sections of private land will be crossed on the way to state land, and the hiker is urged to treat them with respect as continued access is dependent upon how each person uses this privilege.

Day 1 has extremely flat walking. Should the backpacker simply return by the same route, it will indeed be an easy trip; however, the hiker will miss seeing some beautiful forest and several large ponds. Day 2 requires crossing a divide twice. There are a few spots that are slow going with a full backpack, but there are suitable stopping points for lunch, swimming, or fishing, and a relaxed pace should smooth out the trip. Bear in mind that the travel through the woods should be more important to the hiker than the destination.

Access to the trailhead is off Higby Road at Big Moose Lake. Higby Road is 3.9 mi. (6.3 km) from Eagle Bay on the Big Moose Road. It may not have a sign, but it is the first blacktop road to the right you come to and is a prominent intersection. Travel 1.3 mi. (2.1 km) on Higby Road to a parking area in front of a gravel pit on the right side of the road. The posted signs refer to staying out of the pit area. The trailhead is not immediately visible, but if you leave your vehicle you'll find the trail begins at the left side of the grassy clearing.

DAY 1

From the trailhead (0.0 mi.), follow the blue marked trail 100 yds. (92 m) to the privately owned Judson Road. Turn right and walk along this gravel road 0.2 mi. (0.3 km). Just before the road crosses Constable Creek by bridge, an old logging road branches right at a curve in the road.

Turn onto this logging road and continue following blue trail markers. Your course will weave along Constable Creek all the way to its source at Constable Pond. Enroute, the stream has sections that pass through lush vleis and attractive beaver ponds.

A barrier signifying that state land has been reached is seen at 0.3 mi. (0.5 km). The rocky logging road intersects the red marked Hermitage Trail to Queer Lake at 0.5 mi. (0.8 km). Soon after, you leave the road you have been walking on and cross Constable Creek on an interesting rustic bridge.

Reentering private land, the trail is now a most pleasant path beside Constable Creek. Spruce and balsam fir give off fragrant scents. The trail merges with a logging road which enters from the left at 0.9 mi. (1.5 km). Note this junction, since it is easy to miss on the return trip. The grassy road curves back to Constable Creek and crosses it on a large bridge. There is an interesting wooden fish barrier dam across the creek at this point. Its purpose is to keep undesirable, aggressive fish from migrating upstream, where they could affect trout populations in the upper watershed.

Across the bridge, the blue marked trail immediately leaves the road and forks left into the woods. Constable Creek passes through a vlei, beaver dam, and beaver pond, all passed on their right. The Mays Pond trail comes in from the right at 1.3 mi. (2.1 km).

Continuing straight ahead, the trail becomes rocky and footing must be more carefully watched. About fifteen minutes later Constable Pond, more a fair sized lake than a pond, is seen ahead through the trees. Proceeding along the south side of the pond, you find small changes in elevation for the next ten minutes. A small path leads to the shore at one point, just before the Chub Pond junction is reached at 2.5 mi. (4.1 km). Should you continue straight ahead past the junction another 70 yds. (64 m), you will reach the only campsite to be found on this pond. Pigeon Lake and West Mountain are further along the blue marked trail.

The trail to Chub Pond (Lake) follows the yellow marked trail to the right at the junction. (USGS maps in 1903, and other maps until at least 1941 as well as the current DEC *Trails in the Old Forge-Big Moose Region* pamphlet, all call it Chub Pond. The 1954 USGS map and some current DEC trail signs call it Chub Lake. Hikers traditionally call it Chub Pond.)

Rolling terrain gradually gains elevation to a junction at 2.9 mi. (4.7 km). The trail right continues to Queer Lake. Turn left and follow the trail over a knoll and down to the excellent informal campsite on the edge of Chub Pond at 3.1 mi. (5.0 km).

Set in spruces, it would be hard to conjure up a more picturesque setting. A well built fireplace is safely positioned out on the rock shelf that overlooks the pond. This rock gradually slopes into the water, making an ideal entry place for swimming. Across the very large pond a beaver house is seen near the distant shore. Loons cruise silently, keeping a sharp eye on you as they fish.

DAY 2

A midmorning start will get you to Queer Lake in time for a swim before lunch. Leaving the campsite (0.0 mi.), return to the trail junction at 0.2 mi. (0.3 km).

Head south for Queer Lake. At 0.4 mi. (0.6 km), you cross a wide inlet of Chub Pond on an elevated log bridge. A vlei is to the right, and the pond stretches out on your left. You proceed up a moderate grade, rounding the south side of the pond. A good view of the water is seen at 0.6 mi. (1.0 km). The trail descends briefly to a stream crossing and then starts a climb up a moderate grade of some length.

The divide between the Raquette River and the Moose–Black Rivers watersheds is reached at 1.1 mi. (1.8 km). From this height of land a long gradual loss of elevation is found as you continue to Queer Lake. Occasional rises occur, but the general course is a relaxingly easy walk through a marvelous hardwood forest.

The Queer Lake lean-to trail junction is reached at 2.5 mi. (4.1 km). Turn left and drop down to lake level. This red marked trail extends 0.3 mi. (0.5 km) out to the neck of a long peninsula where the lean-to is located. Several opportunities are possible here. It is an ideal place for a swim and lunch break. There is also an interesting walk out to the end of the peninsula, where there are other swimming and camping sites.

Following this rest break, return the 0.3 mi. (0.5 km) to the last trail junction, which now becomes the 3.1 mi. (5.0 km) point of the hike. This time, bear left at the junction and follow yellow markers on generally level terrain to the Mays Pond junction. This is reached at 3.4 mi. (5.5 km).

Turn right at this junction. Again following yellow trail markers, you begin a moderate ascent up a ridge. The early going requires close attention to trail markers. Brushy vegetation and a few blowdowns may cause some concern about the trail ahead. In a few minutes, however, the route improves. It is the least used of the trails you will encounter, and as the hiker use decreases, the wilderness quality of the forest and enjoyment of the hike increases.

The rough climb levels at 3.7 mi. (6.0 km), when you again cross the Raquette River and the Moose–Black Rivers watersheds divide. This is followed by a long, enjoyable, gradual descent to Mays Pond, during which over 300 ft. (92 m) of elevation is lost. This more than compensates for the climb to the height of land you have just completed.

At 4.1 mi. (6.6 km), Mays Pond comes into view. A rocky inlet of the pond is crossed. This large pond is surrounded in this section by thick spruce growth. A few spur trails lead to the water's edge where one can fish or swim. No good camping sites are readily evident along the trail, but some could be made inland a way and up from the shore.

The trail parallels the eastern shore through sweet smelling spruces, before swinging upslope again at 4.3 mi. (7.0 km). This time the climb is shorter, and only a little over 100 ft. (31 m) in elevation is gained before height of land is reached. The trail veers to the left. A gradual drop takes you to the West Mountain trail junction at 5.7 mi. (9.2 km).

Here, you retrace your previously traveled route to the trailhead by turning left and heading for Higby Road. This last level stretch is enjoyable after the climbing and is quite easy. Trailhead is reached at 7.0 mi. (11.3 km).

9. The Santanoni Preserve

Santanoni Preserve Options

Difficulty: Easy
Maps: Newcomb 15′ Series
   Santanoni 15′ Series

The Santanoni Preserve is a good place for beginners to sharpen their backpacking skills. The terrain varies from level to gradual grades for the most part. Most trails follow dirt roads or old logging trails that are slowly closing in as trees encroach.

The story of how the Santanoni Preserve came into state ownership is heartwarming. It reveals what private citizens with high personal ideals for the public good can do when they are well organized. When the preserve was put up for sale, there was great concern that whoever purchased it might greatly alter its use and character. In 1971 the Adirondack Conservancy (a subdivision of the Nature Conservancy) decided to gain control of the property so that it could be resold to the state when financial arrangements could be made. The selling party agreed to sell the property for a little over half its appraised value with the understanding that it would remain in its natural state. A grant from the United States Bureau of Outdoor Recreation was applied for and received. The remaining funds for purchase were raised by the Nature Conservancy and Trout Unlimited. Hence, the land was saved and resold to the state in 1972. It is now part of the Forest Preserve, where it will be forever wild.

Access to the Santanoni Preserve is off Rte. 28N, at the western edge of the village of Newcomb. Turn north at the road junction when you see the Santanoni Preserve sign. Soon after crossing the bridge you arrive at the handsome stone caretaker's building, where you should stop and register, and parking area up the grade at right.

The preserve is used for hiking, fishing, horseback riding, and skiing. Its trails are extremely well suited to cross-country skiing. Hunting is allowed in season. Fishing with artificial lures is permitted from May 1st until September 30th, with special regulations in effect for number and size of fish species.

No special permits for day use or camping are required. The same DEC regulations now apply here as for other state owned land in the Forest Preserve. Designated camp sites are located at Newcomb Lake and Moose Pond. From the gate, it is 4.7 mi. (7.6 km) to Newcomb Lake. Boating is permitted, but no motors are allowed. Moose Pond is 6.0 mi. (9.7 km) from the gate. The connected series of buildings found at Newcomb Lake is not open to the public.

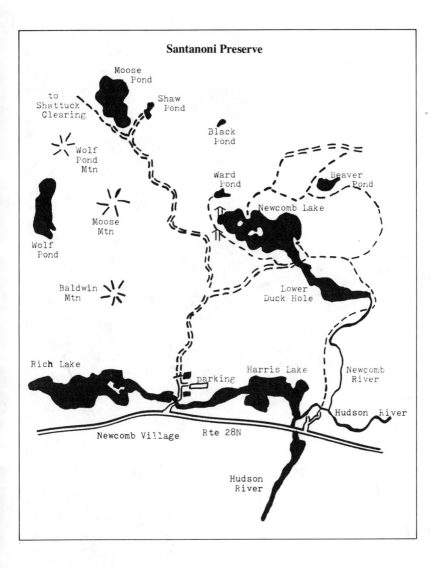

Santanoni Preserve

No specific trips are described here because neither the distances involved nor the hiking routes used are difficult to travel. The Moose Pond Horse Trail continues onward to the Cold River Horse Trail and Shattuck Clearing. It is often used for access into the Cold River country.

Cross-country skiing is excellent throughout the preserve. Snowshoers will find many interesting bushwhacks if they are proficient in their compass skills. It is possible to conduct circuit trips through to Harris Lake along old woods roads.

The Great Range from Mt. Colden

10. High Peaks Wilderness Area

The most physically challenging backpacking in the Adirondack Park is found in the High Peaks Wilderness Area. Before entering this region, it is wise to remember that optimal pleasure comes when the individual's physical stamina matches the toughness of the terrain. Only well conditioned backpackers should take overnight gear into this country. For the many exhausted neophytes who chose the wrong territory to begin their outdoor experiences, blisters, frustration, and often serious injury have often been their only rewards.

It is recommended that the novice to the High Peaks first take a few day hikes to determine the size of the challenge. Carry a light day pack over some of these trails. Then decide how far and over what elevation changes you can haul thirty to forty pounds and still call it fun. This is truly magnificent country, but meet it on terms that are in your favor.

There are three primary points of entry to the High Peaks Wilderness Area. Tahawus is off Rte. 28N in the south near Newcomb. The Garden is a parking area for trails leading through the Johns Brook Valley near the village of Keene Valley on Route 73. The third entry point is outside of Lake Placid, off Rte. 73 at Heart Lake. All three locations are marked with large DEC signposts at the turn-off points from the main highway.

The two trips described here give backpackers a good introduction to the region. If this country proves to suit your fancy, you'll soon purchase a copy of *Guide to Adirondack Trails: High Peaks Region*. This ADK publication has trail descriptions of the whole High Peaks region and includes the ADK topographical trail map, *Trails of the Adirondack High Peak Region*.

It is easy to assume that all manner of help will be available should an emergency occur. After all, at any given time in the summer months, there may be hundreds of hikers spread out through this region. However, there is a vast difference between simply having the presence of numerous individuals and of having qualified, knowledgeable help. Trained personnel for evacuation operations take time to organize. Serious injury may require a dozen or more rescuers or even a helicopter assist from the nearby air force base at Plattsburgh. It is not unusual for twelve to twenty-four hours of time to be required, depending on the weather and the season. Do not take unnecessary chances here. Carry a good first-aid kit and know how to use it.

The last general concern you should have is how to deal with bears. Bears learn to frequent campsites where food is available. Follow the normal procedures discussed elsewhere in this guide to reduce your problems. Do not get careless in this regard. In this high density hiking area, you will encounter bears sooner or later.

There are over 170 mi. (275 km) of foot trails in the High Peaks Wilderness Area. The trails described here vary considerably in terrain, difficulty, and locale. This is intended, so that you may appreciate the enormous potential this region offers to backpackers.

Unless you are in excellent physical condition, you are not advised to try scaling 4000 ft. (1223 m) peaks with full pack. Carry plenty of water. Set a relaxed pace and rest before you become exhausted. A good rule of thumb is to take a fifteen minute break every forty-five minutes. The average rate of travel in the mountains with full pack is 1.5 mi. (2.4 km) per hour, adding one half hour for each 1000 ft. (306 m) elevation gained.

Duck Hole is a relatively easy hike for this country. It provides a more leisurely introduction than the other hike described. The Indian Pass–Lake Colden trip is a step up in difficulty and requires more serious planning.

The Duck Hole Loop

Difficulty: Moderate, with some long grades
Round Trip Distance: 16.6 mi. (26.9 km)
Time Necessary: 2 days
Map: Santanoni 15′ Series or
  Trails of the Adirondack High Peak Region (ADK)

Duck Hole is thought by many to be the most beautiful body of water in the mountains. Deep blue, it sits like a jewel surrounded by green conifers which climb ever higher up the trailless peaks that protect it. Its history, like most Adirondackana, began in the lumber camps of the late 1800s. Loggers cut their way into this region from Long Lake, sixteen miles to the southwest. Camps sprang up at Pine Brook, Shattuck Clearing, and Mountain Pond. The lumberjacks pushed up the Cold River Valley. A dam was built at Duck Hole to back up water for the log runs of spring.

Duck Hole has been a favorite of backpackers since the days of Captain Parker and Mitchel Sabattis. However, an event occurred there in 1978 that riveted the attention of just about everyone in the Adirondacks. The DEC burned to the ground one of its own ranger cabins. A second cabin was razed at Shattuck Clearing. There are few who haven't voiced a definite opinion, one way or the other, on this issue.

In wilderness, man is a visitor. Permanent structures conform neither to the concept nor the legal definition by which wilderness is known to man. Nonetheless, many hikers, hunters, and fishermen have warm memories of those removed cabins and their resident rangers, and long-time hikers recall occasions when help was rendered to those in need. There is surely a greater dimension of wilderness at Duck Hole today in the absence of the cabin and its security. Only a grassy opening, bursting with wild flowers, remains at the beginning of the Roaring Brook Trail to mark the site where the cabin once stood. Duck Hole has become a symbol of the essence of true wilderness in the Adirondacks.

The trail description provided here leads to Duck Hole via Bradley Pond. The return route is via Preston Ponds to the Upper Works at Tahawus.

The trailhead is reached by turning north from Rte. 28N, 7.3 mi. (11.8 km) north of Aiden Lair and approximately 5.3 mi. (8.6 km) east of Newcomb. A

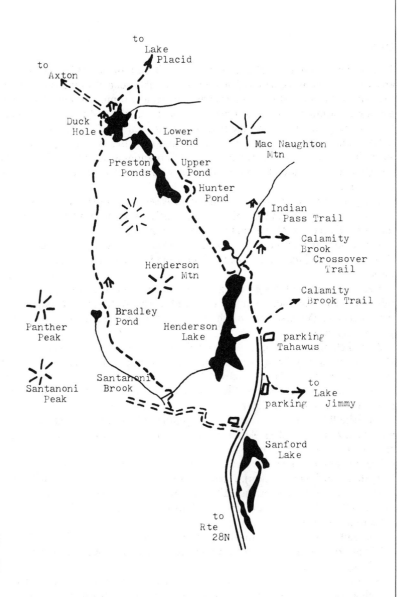

High Peaks Wilderness Area

to
Lake
Placid

to
Axton

Duck
Hole

Lower
Pond

Mac Naughton
Mtn

Preston
Ponds

Upper
Pond

Hunter
Pond

Indian
Pass Trail

Calamity
Brook
Crossover
Trail

Henderson
Mtn

Calamity
Brook Trail

Bradley
Pond

Panther
Peak

Henderson
Lake

parking
Tahawus

Santanoni
Peak

Santanoni
Brook

to
Lake
Jimmy

parking

Sanford
Lake

to
Rte
28N

large DEC signpost marks this road which leads to the National Lead Company titanium mines at Tahawus. Take the left hand fork at the Sanford Lake bridge, 7.6 mi. (12.3 km) from Rte. 28N. Two mi. (3.2 km) north of this bridge, a signpost on the left indicates a parking area.

DAY 1

Trailhead elevation is 1840 ft. (563 m). The trail from the far end of the parking area (0.0 mi.) follows blue DEC markers to a lumber road a short distance along the way. This rough stone road becomes gravel at 1.0 mi. (1.6 km). Gradually gaining elevation, the outlet of Harkness Lake is reached and crossed by bridge. Still climbing, the trail leaves the road and turns right at 1.8 mi. (3.0 km).

The route follows a tributary towards Santanoni Brook. Passing through a grassy lumber clearing, the trail then crosses Santanoni Brook at 2.1 mi. (3.3 km). Swinging left, it gradually ascends the valley between Henderson and Panther mountains.

The grade continues moderately upward. A series of rippling cascades greets you at 3.4 mi. (5.4 km) and 0.1 mi. (0.2 km). Further along the trail, the junction of the closed Santanoni Mountain trail is seen on the left.

A high point of land is crossed at 3.7 mi. (5.9 km). A descent then brings you to a wet area, where a junction at 4.3 mi. (7.6 km) is indicated by yellow paint blazes on trees.

Here, on state land, a legal flagged trail leads left across a beaver dam to the ridge between Santanoni and Panther peaks. The ADK map, "Trails of the Adirondack High Peaks Region," shows the private land boundaries and is a good general reference.

A brief climb then brings you up to the Santanoni Lean-to and height of land. Once called Bradley Pond Lean-to, this is not one of the better shelters found in these mountains. You have traveled 4.4 mi. (7.1 km) and for the first time are off private land and in the Forest Preserve. Your elevation is 2950 ft. (902 m) and height of land is 1110 ft. (339 m) above your starting point.

The next 0.7 mi. (1.1 km) ranges from gradual to steep descents where footing must be carefully watched. At 5.1 mi. (8.3 km) the left fork of the main brook is crossed. The trail then turns to the right.

The rest of the route to Duck Hole is relatively flat. A large tributary is crossed from the left at 5.6 mi. (9.1 km). Ten minutes later, a beaver dam is used to get past a beaver swamp. Soon after, the trail rises a bit above the wet ground. You cross to the east side of the stream at 7.1 mi. (11.5 km) and once again, at 7.8 mi. (12.6 km), cross to the west side.

The trail then tops a ridge and drops down to reach Duck Hole Pond at 7.9 mi. (12.8 km). Hiking upslope from the water's edge, a rock crib dam is negotiated and a spillway dam is reached at 8.2 mi. (13.3 km).

A lean-to and DEC register are found just across the wooden dam. Down the shoreline, 100 yds. (92 m) to the right, a second lean-to is nestled in conifers at the water's edge. In between the two lean-tos an inviting meadow stretches out before you. From it, MacNaughton Mountain can be seen across the pond in the distant east. The whole setting is most picturesque. Elevation of Duck Hole is 2130 ft (651 m).

DAY 2

Upslope from the DEC register, the gravel fire truck road to Axton and Coreys heads westward. It is easy to miss the Roaring Brook Trail that immediately branches northward towards Lake Placid. The small clearing at this junction is where the ranger's cabin was located.

The return route to Tahawus has considerably less elevation change along its course. Consequently, it is generally an easier trail to negotiate. From Duck Hole it is 6.9 mi. (11.2 km) to the Upper Works at Tahawus and another 1.5 mi. (2.4 km) by road back to the parking area from which the trip originated.

The route follows red and blue DEC markers northward along a section of the Northville-Placid Trail and beside Roaring Brook from the fire road junction (0.0 mi.). Easy ups and downs take you near and then away from the stream. Finally, after a few steep pitches, the junction of the Henderson Lake Trail is reached at 0.4 mi. (0.6 km).

Turn right and cross to the east side of Roaring Brook. There may or may not be a bridge to aid you, depending upon whether spring washouts have recently occurred. Following red trail markers, you will soon use a beaver dam to circumvent a beaver bog. You then head up a steep but short slope and pass over a minor ridge. Descending again, you see the northeast bay of Duck Hole at 0.9 mi. (1.5 km).

A few more ups and downs bring you back onto National Lead Company land at 1.1 mi. (1.8 km). A small vlei is crossed, and after a little more climbing Preston Ponds can be seen through the trees to the south.

Corduroy takes you upward again to where the right side of a brook is reached and followed at 1.8 mi. (2.9 km). The remains of the old Piche's lumber camp can be seen at 2.1 mi. (3.4 km), after the brook is crossed. Continuing upstream beside the brook for another fifteen minutes brings you to a beaver pond which may require some minor bushwhacking to get around its east side.

Height of land is reached at 2.5 mi. (4.1 km), where the trail eases through a pass and levels off. You have gained 286 ft. (87 m) since leaving Duck Hole, though the ups and downs may make it seem somewhat greater.

From here you will descend 608 ft. (186 m) to Henderson Lake. A steep pitch at the end of the pass gets you started on your way. Eventually leveling off, the trail rounds Hunter Pond's east side.

Once past the pond, the descent continues, paralleling Hunter Pond outlet. The outlet drains into the Upper Preston Pond. At 3.0 mi. (4.9 km) you reach a trail junction where an unmarked trail leads 60 yds. (55 m) to a private dock on Upper Preston Pond.

Turning sharply left, your trail climbs a short distance up to another pass. (The high ground in this pass is the Hudson–St. Lawrence Rivers Divide. Preston Ponds' drainage will enter the Atlantic through the Gulf of St. Lawrence while outflow from Henderson Lake travels down the Hudson River to New York Bay and the Atlantic.)

Easy traveling is now at hand. At 3.6 mi. (5.8 km) you pass between twin rocks and a gradual descent begins. Following an inlet of Henderson Lake, the boundary line of the Sanford Lake Rod and Gun Club is passed at 3.8 mi. (6.2 km).

After twice crossing the brook the trail leaves the water for a time. Returning, it crosses the stream again and then bypasses a beaver pond on its west side. Once again, at 4.4 mi. (7.1 km), cascades are passed. The brook is crossed two more times, then corduroy takes you through a wet section.

Another junction is reached at 4.7 mi. (7.6 km), where an unmarked trail leads to a private dock near Henderson Lake. Turning abruptly left at this junction, you soon thread your way across a 6 ft. (2 m) high beaver dam, make your way over Indian Pass Brook on a swinging bridge, and arrive at a major trail junction at 5.3 mi. (8.6 km).

To the left, 0.2 mi. (0.3 km) to the north, is Henderson Lean-to. However, your route follows yellow DEC markers to the right (south) toward the Upper Works at Tahawus.

Easy grades take you southward to 5.4 mi. (8.7 km) where the trail merges with a jeep trail. From there it continues a short distance along the jeep road before branching off again in a clearing. Here, it turns sharply left and at 5.6 (9.1 km) starts up an incline, following a tote road. After crossing two brooks, the trail levels and again rejoins the jeep road at 6.5 mi. (10.5 km).

Henderson Lake outlet is crossed on a bridge at 6.7 mi. (10.9 km). A short distance further along, the junction of the Calamity Brook Trail to Lake Colden is passed. Still heading southward, you reach the Upper Works at Tahawus at 6.9 mi. (11.2 km). A very large parking area and two privies are located here.

From this point it is 1.5 mi. (2.4 km) along a blacktop road to the parking area where your trip started. The walk is historically interesting. There was quite a village here until David Henderson had his fatal hunting accident on Calamity Brook in 1845. Henderson had been the guiding force that managed to conquer the economic marketing difficulties of the company. The poor roads and distance from industrial centers made it difficult to be competitive, and the company declined until the needs of the country for titanium and steel revived the area during World War II. The National Lead Company runs mining operations at Tahawus today. Due to the many courtesies of this public spirited company, backpackers have use of many trails which pass over its land to the Forest Preserve beyond.

At 7.4 mi. (12.0 km) a parking area is seen on the left. This is the trailhead for the Opalescent River–Twin Brook Trail to Mount Marcy. At 7.6 mi. (12.3 km) one of the old 1854 MacIntyre Iron Works' furnaces is seen at the roadside. Take a few minutes and examine it. The Bradley Pond–Duck Hole parking area is reached at 8.4 mi. (13.6 km).

Indian Pass—Lake Colden Loop

Difficulty: Varies from moderate to difficult
Rount Trip Distance: 20.6 mi. (33.3 km)
Time Necessary: 3 days with variations
Map: Mount Marcy 15′ Series and
     Santanoni 15′ Series

The Indian Pass– Lake Colden Loop offers an infinite variety of possibilities for shortening, lengthening, toughening, or easing a backpacking trip. The described route is presented because it lends itself to many of these variations. The final trip itinerary is thus left to the whims and desires of the backpacker. One of the more interesting, but not immediately obvious, variations is the so-called "toothbrush hike." You begin at Tahawus and hike through Indian Pass to the Adirondack Mountain Club's Adirondak Loj, where you spend the night. (The Loj came by its unusual spelling due to the phonetic spelling preference of Melville Dewey. This system did not survive as long as did his Dewey Decimal System for cataloging library materials.) The next day you return to Tahawus via Lake Colden. With lunch and bathing suit in your day pack, the only overnight gear you need is a toothbrush. Be sure to make prior reservations at the Loj.

If you have heard of the High Peaks, you've probably heard of Lake Colden. Indian Pass isn't as well known, but it should be. The wild, untamed boulder-ridden gorge, mid-August snow laden caves, and the stupendous thousand foot precipice of Wallface Mountain are natural wonders found nowhere else in the Adirondacks.

Trailhead access is from the Adirondak Loj at Heart Lake. A large DEC sign, "Trail to the High Peaks," 4.0 mi. (6.5 km) southeast of Lake Placid off Route 73, marks the turn-off for Heart Lake. As you travel the open section of the road, you can see the sharp profile of Wallface Mountain at Indian Pass to your right front. To its left is Algonquin, with Avalanche Pass and Lake Colden to its left. Heart Lake, elevation 2178 ft. (666 m), is 4.8 mi. (7.8 km) along Heart Lake Road.

At Heart Lake, meals and lodging can be had at the Loj. A large parking area is available for a small daily use fee, and the public has free use of the Campers and Hikers Building, which provides a source of trail supplies and emergency help when needed.

DAY 1

From the entrance of the public parking area, hike 0.1 mi. (0.2 km) back along Heart Lake Road to the trail sign on the left for Indian Pass. Proceed westward from this junction (0.0 mi), following red DEC trail markers. You soon reach a T-junction, where you make a right turn. Crossing a bridge, you see the trail up Mount Jo to the right. Walk straight ahead around the north shore of Heart Lake. At the end of this pretty little lake, at 0.4 mi. (0.6 km), the old Nye Ski Trail is reached. It was used for the 1932 Olympics.

Continuing to the southwest on the broader red marked trail, you begin to climb as the Forest Preserve boundary is passed. However, the excellent trail is generally quite easy. At 2.1 mi. (3.4 km) a side trail leads 0.3 mi. (0.5 km) to the right to Rocky Falls Lean-to.

Climbing now becomes moderate and a second turn-off to Rocky Falls is passed at 2.3 mi. (3.7 km). After crossing several creeks, Scotts Clearing Lean-to is reached at 3.8 mi. (6.1 km). Turning right, you cross the brook in front of the lean-to.

You soon reach a junction where the foundation of the original Scotts Clearing Lean-to is still evident. Bear right and walk over to Scotts Clearing, a few more yards ahead of you. An enormous old stone dam across Indian Pass Brook and a large camping area are located here. Iroquois Peak is visible straight ahead as you enter this old lumber camp clearing. This is a very attractive spot and good place to take a long rest break before beginning the hard climb ahead. The trail to Scott and Wallface Ponds begins at the far end of the dam and makes a good side trip for people who camp here.

From the dam, the original route followed up the east side of Indian Pass Brook. However, the beavers know a good thing when they see one. In recent years they've repaired the stone dam, and the result has been a flooded Low Water Route most of the year. It is suggested that you return to the junction by the old lean-to foundation and take the High Water Route around the obstacle.

From the old lean-to foundation, continue straight ahead. At 4.1 mi. (6.6 km) another trail from the clearing enters from the right. Some stiff climbing ensues for a short while to a height of land where a moderate descent takes you back toward the brook. Avoid any other side trails that enter. There is a splendid view of the old dam through the trees. After reaching a second height of land, you make a rather steep descent to rejoin the Lower Water Route at 4.5 mi. (7.3 km).

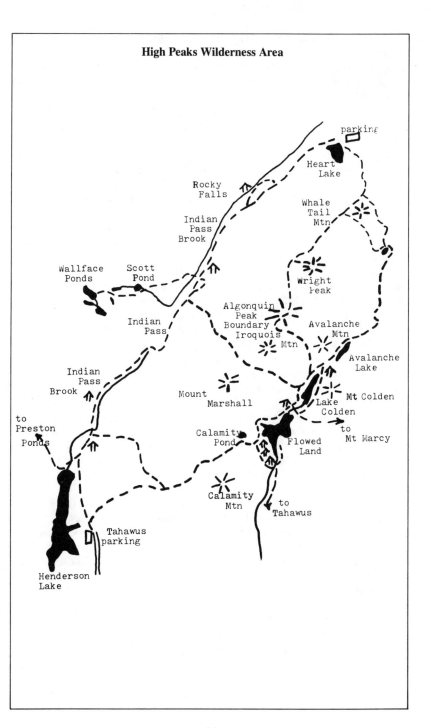

High Peaks Wilderness Area

parking

Heart
Lake

Rocky
Falls

Whale
Tail
Mtn

Indian
Pass
Brook

Wright
Peak

Wallface
Ponds

Scott
Pond

Algonquin
Peak
Boundary
Iroquois
Mtn

Avalanche
Mtn

Indian
Pass

Avalanche
Lake

Indian
Pass
Brook

Mount
Marshall

Lake
Colden

Mt Colden

to
Preston
Ponds

Calamity
Pond

Flowed
Land

to
Mt Marcy

Calamity
Mtn

to
Tahawus

Tahawus
parking

Henderson
Lake

The trail then parallels Indian Pass Brook, crossing both tributaries and brook frequently. At 4.9 mi. (8.1 km) the crossover Algonquin Pass Trail between Iroquois Peak and Mount Marshall enters from the left. This 3.3 mi. (5.4 km) trail terminates near the Lake Colden ranger station. It is very steep, ascending 1260 ft. (385 m) enroute.

From this point, climbing becomes very rugged, though the Adirondack 46'ers greatly improved the trail with several ladders in 1980. Take your time and rest when necessary.

After two more stream crossings, the trail narrows and steepens. Climbing over and around large boulders, some 400 ft. (122 m) vertical ascent occurs in the next 0.4 mi. (0.6 km). The trail finally levels just before reaching height of land. Look for ice caverns in the deepest parts of this section. Refreshing drafts of cool air stream out of them even in August.

At 5.5 mi. (8.9 km), a DEC sign indicates the high point of the pass has been reached. Elevation is 2834 ft. (867 m). This is some 656 ft. (201 m) above Heart Lake.

By this time, most hikers will have begun to be somewhat awe inspired. Even the blockhouse size boulders, ice caverns, and rugged trail don't prepare you for the marvelous cliffs of Wallface Mountain. It's no surprise that in 1840 Ebenezer Emmons stated in his first *Natural History Survey of the Adirondacks* that he was more impressed by "the view of the simple naked rock of Adirondack Pass (Indian Pass)" than he had been previously by Niagara Falls. This imposing rock wall increasingly rivets your attention as you proceed and as its relative position changes with respect to the trail.

The trail dips a little, rises, and finally begins a gradual descent past unbelievably gigantic boulders. At 6.0 mi. (9.1 km) you reach Summit Rock. A very short side trail to the right takes you over a rocky incline to a broad sloping ledge. Here an extremely fine view down the valley toward Henderson Lake presents itself. Behind you are the cliffs of Wallface Mountain, and across the valley to your right stretches Wallface Mountain. In the far distance down the valley Santanoni Mountain, Panther Peak, and Henderson Mountain reach into the sky. Take a long rest break here and enjoy the vista.

From Summit Rock the trail descends steeply. In the next 0.5 mi. (0.8 km) you will lose 450 ft (138 m) elevation. Ladders occasionally appear and are used to get by the immense boulders found here. At 6.5 mi. (10.5 km) you cross Indian Pass Brook. (This Indian Pass Brook flows into Lake Henderson; do not confuse it with the Indian Pass Brook on the opposite side of the pass, which flows into the West Branch of the Ausable River.)

The trail levels somewhat. It recrosses Indian Pass Brook, various tributaries, and the outlet of Wallface Pond. Finally, at 7.7 mi. (12.5 km), Wallface Lean-to is reached on the right bank of Indian Pass Brook.

It is recommended that you camp here for the night. Henderson Lean-to is another 1.0 mi. (1.6 km) further down the trail.

From Wallface Lean-to, continue down the pass. At 0.6 mi. (1.0 km) the trail squeezes between two enormous boulders. The Indian Pass–Calamity Brook Crossover is soon reached in an old lumber clearing, at 0.7 mi. (1.1 km). Upper Works at Tahawus is 2.1 mi. (3.4 km) straight ahead.

Turn left and follow blue DEC trail markers eastward. The trail follows and then crosses a brook several times as the grade gradually increases to moderate levels of incline. A col at the top of the ridge is reached at 1.6 mi. (2.6 km). The elevation here is 2430 ft. (743 m); your ascent has been about 500 ft. (167 m) from the junction.

A few minutes after starting down the opposite side of the ridge a grassy meadow and small brook are reached. This brook also will be crossed several times until the trail finally swings away from it. A low ridge is climbed and descent begins again. You pass the Forest Preserve boundary, and reenter private land at 2.3 mi. (3.7 km).

The route becomes steeper and soon a beaver swamp appears. It is circumvented to a great extent by climbing around its western edge; near its outlet, the swamp is crossed on logs. The trail then winds along a logging road for a ways before rising to drier ground. A few more minutes of walking brings you to the Calamity Brook trail junction at 2.8 mi. (4.5 km). Upper Works at Tahawus is reached by crossing the bridge over Calamity Brook and hiking 1.7 mi. (2.8 km) to the west.

Still following the blue marked trail, turn left and head upstream along the brook. A secondary stream is crossed before the trail joins an abandoned tote road. In a series of moderate grades and intervening level sections the trail begins a lengthy ascent. A short drop in elevation then brings you down steeply to a suspension bridge at 3.9 mi. (6.3 km).

Climbing again commences to height of land, where at 4.8 mi. (7.8 km) you head downward a short ways to Calamity Pond. At the far end of the pond, a short trail leads to the pond's edge where an interesting monument is located. It was placed on this spot by the children of David Henderson who, while on a hunting trip in 1845, accidently shot himself here. Hence, the name Calamity Pond.

The trail continues with few ups and downs to the shore of the Flowed Lands at 5.3 mi. (8.6 km). Far down the flow, Mount Colden rises in the distance, with its naked shoulders profiled against the open sky. The two Calamity Brook lean-tos are found here and Flowed Lands Lean-to is a few minutes walk down the red marked trail to the right.

The Flowed Land was drained in late summer 1980 so that the deteriorating dam at its outlet could be inspected. When filled with water, the view of Mount Colden from the southern end of Flowed Land is one of the most beautiful in the mountains. If left in its drained state to become a meadow, the view will also be beautiful for many years until trees grow in and close it off. Whether to remove or to repair the dam is but one of the difficult decisions that must be made concerning the High Peaks Wilderness Area in the next few years. The dam at Lake Colden was replaced in the summer of 1980 after washing out the previous spring during meltoff.

The Lake Colden and Marcy Dam areas are heavily used in the summer months. There are enforced restrictions placed upon the number of campers permitted to camp overnight in these two areas. While the hiker usually has no difficulty finding an open lean-to or a designated tenting site, it is advisable to avoid bypassing an available site when the hour is late in the afternoon. Don't try to squeeze out that extra mile or two or you may be walking half the night trying to find another open spot.

For purposes of this trail description, Day 2 will continue to the ranger's cabin at Lake Colden. It is assumed, however, that campers will select an overnight camping spot at some point between Flowed Lands and the cabin.

From the Flowed Lands shore, turn left and cross the bridge over Calamity Brook's outlet into the Flowed Lands. Several informal campsites are in this immediate area just over the bridge. An easy hiking route follows red trail markers 0.4 mi. (0.6 km) to where it climbs over a low ridge.

A rocky section takes you down again to lake level. Herbert Brook is crossed at 6.1 mi. (9.9 km). (Herbert Brook is the usual ascent route up trailless Mount Marshall.) Not far past this brook, the McMartin Lean-to can be seen across the Opalescent River to the right. It can often be reached by rock hopping the river.

Another low ridge and then a swampy area are crossed. At 6.4 mi. (10.4 km), the rocky edge above the crib dam at Lake Colden outlet is reached. This is a major trail junction on the route up Mount Marcy. There are more lean-tos across the dam. These are reached by descending the ladder, crossing the outlet dam, and then crossing the crib dam over the Opalescent to another trail junction. There, the yellow trail leads to three lean-tos on the southeast shore of Lake Colden. The trail to the right of this junction leads to three lean-tos on the Opalescent River.

Continuing along the west side of Lake Colden, you now follow blue trail markers. West Lean-to is reached at 6.5 mi. (10.5 km), and 53 yds. (48 m) further on is Beaver Point Lean-to. Side trails lead to both lean-tos. Magnificent views of Mount Colden are seen as you climb over the small Beaver Point promontory. Designated tent sites are found in the area ahead. Tenting may be done only at such sites.

The way is along the lake shore. A small bog is crossed just before the trail passes in front of the ranger's cabin at 6.9 mi. (11.2 km). This is the only ranger cabin in the Adirondacks which is manned throughout the winter months (1980).

DAY 3

From the ranger's cabin (0.0 mi.) the blue marked trail heads northward towards Marcy Dam. Avoid the crossover trail to Indian Pass via Algonquin Pass that begins near the ranger's cabin. Cold Brook is crossed on a bridge, and the trail junction with the Algonquin Peak trail is reached at 0.2 mi. (0.3 km). Continuing along the shoreline, a side trail to Caribou Lean-to is seen on the right at 0.6 mi. (1.0 km). Thirty yds. (28 m) further on, after crossing the outlet of Avalanche Lake, the trail junction with the trail from the east side of Lake Colden is reached.

Continue northward towards Avalanche Lake, now following yellow trail markers. The trail heads along the left bank of the outlet, recrossing the outlet at 0.9 mi. (1.5 km) just as Avalanche Lake is approached.

The next 0.5 mi. (0.8 km) is somewhat rough as you scamper over boulders, travel up and down ladders, and perform other nimble-footed tasks while trying not to fall into the lake. On a bridge at 1.1 mi. (1.8 km), one can clearly see the trap dike up Mount Colden across the lake. It offers a challenging route up this formidable peak. Then, at 1.2 mi. (1.9 km), the famous "Hitch-Up-Matilda" bridge is reached. Today, a bridge is firmly bolted to the walls of the pass, but back over a century ago Mr. Fielding kept urging his wife, Matilda, to "Hitch-Up" as Guide Bill Nye struggled to carry her through this then bridgeless section without getting her wet. The upper end of the lake is reached at 1.4 mi. (2.3 km). Soon after, a rock shelter is seen on the right.

As the climb up to the col begins, the walls of the pass close in on you even more. It is a unique experience to thread your way along this narrowing trail. At 2.0 mi. (3.2 km), height of land is reached. Here, the way levels for awhile before beginning the longer descent of over 600 ft. (183 m) to Marcy Dam.

A winter ski trail weaves in and out of this route. Moderate slopes switchback their way downward. A tote road is joined and then the trail parallels the right bank of a tributary of Marcy Brook. Telephone line from the ranger cabin is seen. A wet area is passed on a long log walk.

The junction of the Lake Arnold Crossover trail is reached at 2.5 mi. (4.1 km). In a large clearing are the two Avalanche Pass lean-tos. The trail passes by the lean-tos and crosses Marcy Brook on a wide bridge at the opposite end of the clearing. Turning left, you encounter gradual grades which carry you along at a relaxing pace. In winter the run from the top of Avalanche Pass to Marcy Dam is an outstanding ski route.

Another lean-to is reached at 2.9 mi. (4.7 km), and the trail meets the right bank of Marcy Brook at 3.2 mi. (5.2 km). Leveling off, the trail reaches Marcy Dam at 3.6 mi. (5.8 km). There are eight lean-tos, large group tenting areas, and other designated camping spots here.

Bear left as the blue marked Van Hoevenberg trail to Marcy merges with your trail from the right. The holding dam for logs during past times is reached at 3.8 mi. (6.2 km). A trail register and ranger's cabin are located beside the dam. A water spigot is found at the base of the dam on the outflow side. Standing on the walk across the dam on an early autumn morning when frost covers the mountain tops and the colored reflections of thousands of trees are seen in the water is an incomparable experience.

At the far end of the dam, the Van Hoevenberg trail turns right, climbing a rise as it begins the remaining 2.2 mi. (3.6 km) to the Adirondak Loj.

You drop down the rise to the rocky edge of Marcy Brook at 4.1 mi. (6.6 km). The trail then meanders gently over several knolls. A bridge with a railing is crossed at 4.5 mi. (7.3 km). A trail junction is reached at 5.0 mi. (8.1 km). The route to the left heads up Algonquin Peak. Straight ahead is the old route to the Loj.

Turn right and follow the new route (1973) above the right bank of MacIntyre Brook. A moderate grade takes you down to a crossing of the brook at 5.6 mi.

(9.1 km). A second brook is crossed before you join the Hicks trail (bear right) for a short ways. Follow blue trail signs.

You climb a moderately steep grade which takes you to the DEC register and lower parking area at 6.0 mi. (9.7 km). The Campers and Hikers Building is directly ahead of you at the opposite end of the clearing.

11. The Five Ponds Wilderness Area

When the state built Stillwater Reservoir, the flooded lands blocked off access to a huge section of William Seward Webb's lumbering acreage. The state purchased it in compensation, and it thus became part of the Forest Preserve. Consequently there is today a tract of virgin pine, never lumbered or burned, within the Five Ponds Wilderness Area.

Canoers have long known Cranberry Lake and the Oswegatchie River, but for some reason backpackers have been slow to enter this region in appreciable numbers. It is in many ways unique, which is why folks in the St. Lawrence River country continue to come to their "South Woods" for relaxation and self-renewal.

Hikers wishing a more comprehensive description of trails will find the ADK *Guide to Adirondack Trails: Northern Region,* by Peter O'Shea, and the ADK map "Trails of the Northern Region" to be helpful.

Cowhorn Pond—High Falls Loop

Difficulty: Easy walking, but long.
Round Trip Distance: 18.0 mi. (29.2 km)
Time Necessary: 2 long or 3 short days
Maps: Cranberry Lake 15' Series or
**   Five Ponds 7.5' Series and**
Wolf Mountain 7.5' Series

The trail options on this trip include a short overnighter at Janacks Landing, a side trip up Cat Mountain, and an infinite number of ponds to visit. The circuit could take two weeks if you combined the Five Ponds route with it. The outing described here can be a two day trip for backpackers who like to push it or a leisurely three day trip for those who want some fishing or plan to study the "plains" area.

Access to the trailhead is from the village of Wanakena, off Rte. 3 between Star Lake and Cranberry Lake. From Rte. 3, drive 1.0 mi. (1.6 km) south to Wanakena. Bear right at any road forks you come to along the way. A bridge takes you over the Oswegatchie River. From there, travel 0.5 mi. (0.8 km) to a small DEC sign on the right side of the road indicating the Dead Creek Fire Road. There is a parking area on the right, a few meters beyond the sign and gate.

DAY 1

From the gate (0.0 mi.), follow the fire road to its end. Red trail markers guide you along the almost level grassy route. After about twenty-five minutes of walking, a vlei is passed. A few minutes later you catch your first glimpse of Dead Creek Flow on the left. Your position now is almost at the end of the

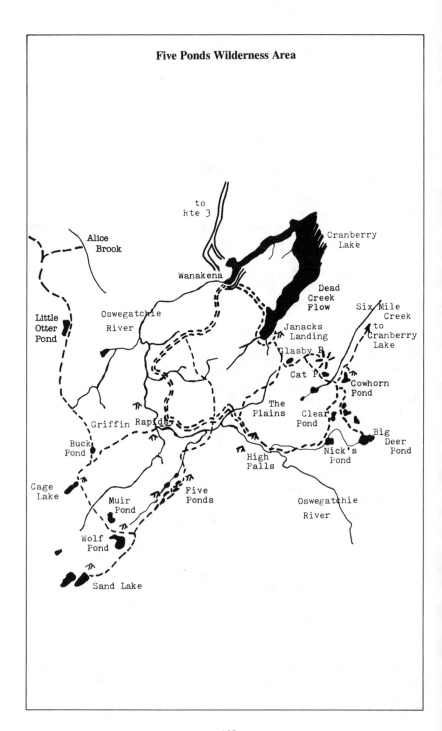

Five Ponds Wilderness Area

to
Rte 3

Alice
Brook

Cranberry
Lake

Wanakena

Dead
Creek
Flow

Little
Otter
Pond

Oswegatchie
River

Six Mile
Creek
to
Cranberry
Lake

Janacks
Landing

Glasby R

Cat P

Cowhorn
Pond

The
Plains

Clear
Pond

Griffin Rapids

Buck
Pond

Big
Deer
Pond

Cage
Lake

Nick's
Pond

High
Falls

Oswegatchie
River

Muir
Pond

Five
Ponds

Wolf
Pond

Sand Lake

narrow bay of Cranberry Lake. At 2.0 mi. (3.2 km) the fire road ends. There is a picnic table and fireplace here by the shore of the flow.

A trail bears right, around the end of the flow, and crosses two inlets on log bridges. The route soon moves away from the water and enters hardwoods. At 3.2 mi. (5.2 km) a trail junction is reached. The left hand turn leads 0.2 mi. (0.3 km) to Janacks Landing, where a lean-to and several good tent sites are found on the shore of Dead Creek Flow.

Hiking straight ahead from the junction, you still continue to follow red trail markers. The route is flat for about fifteen minutes, then you enter a narrow draw and begin a gradual ascent. A spring is seen below the left bank of the trail, as the steeper grade begins. Near the end of the draw, the grade becomes moderately steep as you climb to height of land.

Just past height of land a junction is reached at 4.0 mi. (6.5 km). This trail fork could easily be missed if you were not looking for it. The "plains trail" continues down the slope, following blue trail markers.

Turn left at this fork and follow the contour along the side of the ridge. The sound of rushing water is heard as you approach the cascading outlet of Glasby Pond. The trail follows the right bank of the stream. A bridge takes you across the outlet just before you reach the pond at 4.3 mi. (7.0 km). Glasby Pond, with blueberry bushes surrounding its shores, is most attractive. Its dark waters and the slopes of Cat Mountain across the pond create a primitive setting.

The trail swings by an informal campsite, gains a little elevation, and continues around the south side of the pond. Take time to admire the water as you walk along.

Now heading away from the pond, you slowly gain elevation. At 4.5 mi. (7.3 km) the Cat Mountain trail junction is reached. The trail straight ahead leads 0.6 mi. (1.0 km) up Cat Mountain. This is a very easy climb and is well worth the effort, for the view is excellent.

Turning right from this junction, head southeast and follow yellow trail markers towards Cowhorn Junction. A leaf covered trail over low rolling grades provides comfortable walking. It doesn't seem long before you pass some large boulders and notice Cat Mountain Pond to your left at 5.6 mi. (9.1 km). The trail stays well back from the shore of this attractive body of water. Unmarked paths occasionally lead to the shoreline.

At 6.1 mi. (9.9 km) Six Mile Creek, the outlet of Bassout Ponds, is crossed on a log bridge. Soon a moderately steep rise takes you up to the top of an esker ridge where Cowhorn Junction is located at 6.5 mi. (10.5 km). Large Cowhorn Pond is seen through the trees far below you to the east.

Turn left at this junction and walk along the top of the ridge, a narrow spine with drop-offs on both sides, to the north. Tall hemlocks and pleasant breezes create an unusually enjoyable section of trail. Another junction is reached at the end of Cowhorn Pond at 6.9 mi. (11.2 km). The trail straight ahead leads 3.8 mi. (6.2 km) to the South Flow on Cranberry Lake.

Take the right fork around the shoreline 0.2 mi. (0.3 km) to Cowhorn Pond Lean-to, reached at 7.1 mi. (11.5 km). It sits in a large open clearing, back from the water. There is a sweeping view of the pond from the shelter.

DAY 2

From the Cowhorn Pond Lean-to (0.0 mi.), hike 0.6 mi. (1.1 km) back to Cowhorn Junction on top of the ridge. From there, continue straight past the junction a short distance to an unmarked junction, where there is an informal campsite with a stone fireplace. The left fork continues to follow yellow markers 2.0 mi. (3.2 km) past several ponds to Big Deer Pond. It was here that the famous hermit guide Fide (Philo) Scott, the prototype Irving Batcheller used when he wrote *Silas Strong, Emperor of the Woods* in 1906, once lived.

Bear right at this fork and follow red trail markers to High Falls. This section shows much evidence of its glacial past. A gradual downgrade takes you along a shallow pass for some distance. The woods open a bit and a small esker-like ridge is seen on the left. A clearing is then passed on the right, just before the trail closes in on you quite abruptly. Before you realize it, you have reached the shore of pretty little Clear Pond at 1.6 mi. (2.6 km).

The trail may seem to disappear here, but if you turn right and follow the edge of the clearing the trail soon becomes obvious again. You will see an old trail sign nailed to a tree. Avoid an unmarked path at 2.2 mi. (3.6 km). which drops down a knoll to the left. Your route swings up over the knoll and leads down to an informal campsite. The trail closes in again just before reaching Nick's Pond at 2.4 mi. (3.9 km). A few informal campsites are found here, but there is little to keep you from continuing along the trail. Nick's Pond must be considered an emergency camping spot at best.

The section between Nick's Pond and Pine Ridge has several low wet spots, where ground draining to the Oswegatchie River must be traversed. With care, the hiker can keep his feet dry most times of the year, but some people might prefer to put on an old pair of sneakers and plow right through the wet spots.

At 4.0 mi. (6.5 km) you begin noticing very large white pine trees as you cross over a low ridge. This is Pine Ridge. The November 25, 1950, hurricane knocked down many of the giants, but it is still a most impressive stand of virgin timber, well worth observing.

You cross Nick's Pond Outlet again before climbing a moderate grade ridge. A rocky stream is then crossed and the trail levels. An informal campsite is seen on the high bank of the Oswegatchie River as you approach High Falls, and a lean-to soon appears on the left. The trail continues to a junction with the High Falls Truck Road at 5.3 mi. (8.9 km), a few meters from High Falls.

High Falls is the furthest upstream on the Oswegatchie River that a canoe can be paddled without portage. It has long been a favorite trout fishing and camping spot, and at one time there was a sportsmen's camp here. Today, a lean-to is on the right bank above the beautiful falls. A large bridge permits you to reach a second lean-to on the left bank below the falls. It is a magnificent setting. Please take special care to carry out your litter and observe good camping techniques while here so that all may enjoy it.

This is a perfect place for a lunch break and swim if you are pushing on. Overnight campers can set up camp, do some fishing or perhaps visit "the plains" in the afternoon.

The route from High Falls follows the High Falls Truck Road 0.8 mi. (1.3 km) to a trail junction with the "plains" trail. The trail straight ahead leads 1.0 mi. (1.6 km) to the junction of the Leary Trail with the Five Ponds Trail.

The plains used to be called Cornelius Carter's Plains after an early guide who lived there. The origin of the plains is not known, but some people feel it may have been a large crown fire that made these soils so sterile. If so, no records of such a fire exists. Others believe an extreme variation in water table level keeps the plains in its open state. Whatever the cause, the open ground is covered with berry bushes and occasional groupings of white pine and tamarack trees. It is a most interesting area.

Turn right and head out onto the plains. Glasby Creek, the outlet of Glasby Pond, will be crossed three different times as you cross this section of trail. After its third crossing, this blue markered trail gains elevation. Glasby Pond Junction is reached at 8.3 mi. (13.4 km).

From here, the reverse of the earlier trail description is followed back to Wanakena. The gate and parking area are reached at 12.3 mi. (19.9 km).

Five Ponds—Cage Lake Loop

Difficulty: Easy grades, but uneven trail conditions.
Round Trip Distance: 21.8 mi. (35.3 km)
Time Necessary: 3 days, more with options.
Maps: Cranberry Lake & Oswegatchie 15′ Series
   or Five Ponds & Wolf Pond 7.5′ Series

The Five Ponds– Cage Lake Loop is a true wilderness backpacking trip. While campers frequently head for the lean-to at Big Shallow, relatively few hikers go on to Sand Lake. Beavers have made the full circuit to Cage Lake more difficult, but for those who want the essence of true wilderness, the Five Ponds–Cage Lake Loop can't be beat.

The trip isn't recommended for beginners or those who feel squeamish about crossing a bridge that happens to be underwater. In places, the distance will seem greater than it really is. It isn't a region to rush through.

Side trips to Sand Lake and Alice Brook are possible. If going to Sand Lake, it might be wise to spend the night there and add a day to the trip. The Alice Brook excursion is more of a half-day affair. Give yourself plenty of time here and plan your daily trip distances carefully.

Access to the trailhead is from the village of Wanakena. Follow the same access directions given for the Cowhorn Pond–High Falls Loop to the bridge over the Oswegatchie River at Wanakena. The High Falls Truck Trail, where you begin to hike, is 0.1 mi. (0.2 km) past this bridge, on the right. Continue a short distance past this dirt road to a tennis court. Just beyond the tennis court is a parking area.

DAY 1

The trail follows red DEC trail markers to a gate 0.1 mi. (0.2 km) along the truck road. The very flat route passes a pond that is on the left. The slightly raised road has shallow water on both sides in places before it begins to climb at 0.9 mi. (1.5 km). As you climb the gradual grade, Skate Creek can be seen through the trees below you to the right.

A spring on the left, by a boulder, is a good place to fill up before leaving the road. Not much further ahead is the junction for the Leary Trail. At 1.5 mi. (2.4 km), a signpost marks the location where the blue marked trail heads up the slope to the left.

From the junction, the moderate sloped trail rises more than 260 ft. (80 m) before passing over the eastern shoulder of High Rock at 2.1 mi. (3.4 km). The middle part of this trail coincides with the old Albany Trail as it descends about 100 ft. (31 m) to a swampy area and stream crossing at 3.0 mi. (4.9 km). Beaver activity may cause temporary inconvenience before a gradual grade takes you over the lower shoulder of the west side of Roundtop Mountain. An easy drop in elevation brings you to a four way junction as you rejoin the High Falls Truck Trail at 4.2 mi. (6.8 km). Taking the Leary Trail saves about 0.7 mi. (1.1 km) of walking compared to staying on the truck road to this road junction.

Moving straight across the truck road, the blue marked trail leads southward towards Five Ponds. After fifteen minutes of walking along this route, you'll see a path on the left. It leads to a very nice informal campsite with a fireplace at the base of a large boulder. The main trail curves around a slope to a bridge over the Oswegatchie River. Another path, near the bridge, also heads to the campsite. Across the bridge is a second, less desirable, campsite.

At 5.5 mi. (8.9 km) the trail makes an abrupt left-hand turn at a junction. Avoid the right side of this junction, which will take you northward to the Oswegatchie River.

A series of log bridges and corduroy takes you through a wet section in good shape. The outlet of Five Ponds is on the right and is soon crossed. You briefly climb away from the stream but soon return. The rocky stream is attractive. The route is now squeezed between the water and the steepening wall of the Five Ponds esker at your right.

At 6.7 mi. (10.9 km) the trail comes to a shallow ford at the outlet of Big Shallow. Bearing right, along the stream shore, you almost immediately reach the lean-to on this pond. The lean-to stands at the shore with a nice view across the water. A spring is found a short distance along the path around the right side of the pond. A bushwhack up the side of the esker, past the spring, is a worthwhile venture. Mammoth white pines are found there. You may also want to walk southward along the crest of the esker, where you can drop down to Big Five, or walk northward on the crest, where you can drop down to Little Five. Both of these ponds are on the opposite side of the esker from the lean-to.

Big Shallow Lean-to is a good spot to spend the night. If it's occupied, however, the trip to the Little Shallow lean-to isn't very far.

DAY 2

From the Big Shallow Lean-to (0.0 mi.), return the short distance to the ford across the outlet of the pond. Cross this creek and climb up the minor grade onto higher ground. About ten minutes later, the route passes between tiny Washbowl on the left and Little Shallow on the right. Popping over a small ridge brings you to the Little Shallow Lean-to at 0.5 mi. (0.8 km). It sits well up from the water and would be a good choice during black fly season. There is a spring down near the pond.

The trail continues on past the lean-to. It climbs very gradually. Soon the trail enters a narrow valley, where a beaver pond is situated. Thereafter, the route levels for a while before resuming the long gradual climb through the still narrow valley. Reaching height of land, the course descends gradually for some distance before the valley finally widens out a bit.

About ten minutes later, you climb over a small rise and drop down to the Wolf Pond junction at 2.1 mi. (3.4 km). The left fork leads 2.6 mi. (4.2 km) to Sand Lake. Good fishing, a long sandy beach, and a fine lean-to are good reasons to spend a night at Sand Lake if you have the time. This would be 4.1 mi. (7.6 km) from Big Shallow Lean-to.

Take the right fork for Wolf Pond, now following yellow DEC trail markers. Easy walking lets you quickly cover the 0.6 mi. (1.0 km) to Wolf Pond Lean-to, reached at 2.7 mi. (4.4 km). Wolf Pond is a very sizeable sheet of water. One of the idiosyncrasies of Adirondackana is that a body of water's being called a pond or a lake seems to have little to do with its size. By any normal standards, this is a pretty good sized lake.

The lean-to sits two or three minutes' walk above Wolf Pond. Large white pines dominate the scene. A side trail behind the lean-to takes you to a spring. It is difficult to get clean water from the pond itself, as it has a rather murky shoreline. A walk down to the shore is most rewarding, however, because the expanse is almost panoramic in scope.

From the lean-to the trail swings right, over a small knoll. It then descends to a wide open valley, through which runs the outlet of Wolf Pond. Currently, crossing this vale has presented no problems. However, in the recent past, beaver activity completely flooded the area knee deep with water.

Trail markers exist but are hard to find. The area of possible flooding is only 100 yds. (31 m) long. If the route is not obvious, take a northwest heading on your compass and head out towards the opposite side. Trail markers can be found as high ground is reached.

After making your way over to the far side of the valley, you negotiate a moderate slope on dry ground. The character of the woods begins to change as you reach higher ground. Better soil drainage lets the birches, maples, and beeches grow in abundance.

At about 3.2 mi. (5.2 km) you drop down the steep bank and cross the outlet of Muir Pond. Climbing the opposite bank, you continue through a fine hardwood forest on a comfortable trail.

A gradual loss of elevation brings you to the outlet of Deer Marsh at 3.6 mi. (5.8 km). As you continue northeastward, easy terrain eventually brings you within sight of Cage Lake. Walking near the shoreline for 0.1 mi. (0.2 km), you reach the Cage Lake Lean-to at 5.5 mi. (8.9 km).

The lean-to is a newer prefabricated type, which DEC airdropped onto the site. It sits up a little ways from the lake. A good view of the lake can be had from the clearing. The lake is to the left of the lean-to's front. The hiking trail leads straight ahead down a steep enbankment to the lake's outlet stream, where good drinking water is found. The refreshing breeze off the lake and the possibility of a cooling swim make this a good place to spend the night. At the height of the black fly season, on June 22, 1976, Joan Dean left a message on the lean-to ceiling for future hikers to ponder: "There is a rare beauty here that makes it worth the bugs." It is even more enjoyable in August, when there are no bugs.

DAY 3

In earlier editions of this guide, Day 3 of this trip took you from Cage Lake past Buck Pond, to the lean-to above Griffin Rapids on the Oswegatchie River, and then to the High Falls Truck Road. The bridge across the river at the lean-to collapsed and there are no plans to replace it. It is possible to go as far as the lean-to (3.3 mi. or 5.3 km), though beaver activity may be a problem. To make a circuit, Day 3 now runs past Buck Pond and out to the Youngs Road trailhead, 1.4 mi. (2.3 km) from NY 3 in Star Lake village.

From Cage Lake lean-to (0.0 mi.), the trail crosses the outlet of Cage Lake on rocks. After a short spell on high ground, it drops to a low, wet area. Well corduroyed and bridged, passage is not difficult, though there is slow going for awhile.

Finally, gradual grades take you to higher ground again. After continuing on the level for a few minutes, another grade takes you up to the Buck Pond Trail junction. The trail you have been following continues on to the Oswegatchie River lean-to. You should bear left and head for Buck Pond.

The Buck Pond Trail swings around the west side of Buck Pond and follows yellow DEC trail markers. A junction is reached at 1.5 mi. (2.4 km) at the north end of the pond. The two camps on this private in-holding water are near the shore. The hiking trail continues northward.

Elevation increases gradually until you reach a hemlock covered hill at 2.6 mi. (4.2 km), and then quickly drops down to the Post-Henderson Railroad bed at 3.4 mi. (5.5 km). The route follows the trackless remains of this old logger's railroad for the next four miles.

The firm course provides level walking, except at a difficult crossing of a beaver flow at 3.8 mi. (6.2 km). Then, at 5.3 mi. (8.6 km), Little Otter Pond Outlet is crossed, as a balsam growth vlei is negotiated. The outlet is again crossed at 6.4 mi. (10.4 km), as the trail approaches Little Otter Pond.

The trail passes along the east shore of the pond, on its northward trek. At 7.4 mi. (12.0 km), the railroad bed continues on, but the trail bears left from it. (It is possible to extend this hike by continuing along the railroad bed another 2.0 mi.

[3.2 km] until it intersects the Alice Brook Trail and then walking that trail 0.9 mi. [1.5 km] back to the Buck Pond Trail at a point 0.5 mi. [0.8 km] from Youngs Road.)

Now off the hardened railroad bed, the Buck Pond Trail is deeply rutted from use as a jeep trail and is less pleasant. A jeep trail enters from the left at 7.6 mi. (12.3 km) and the route continues through hardwood forest over rolling terrain.

The Alice Brook Trail branches right, at a junction at 9.1 mi. (14.7 km). (It leads 1.1 mi. [1.8 km] to Alice Brook.)

Finally, at 9.6 mi. (15.6 km), the trail reaches the trailhead at the east side of Youngs Road, near a green camp, and diagonally across the road from the Star Lake–Streeter Trail. This is just south of the metal bridge crossing Little River and is 1.4 mi. (2.3 km) from the Youngs Road intersection with NY 3 at Star Lake village.

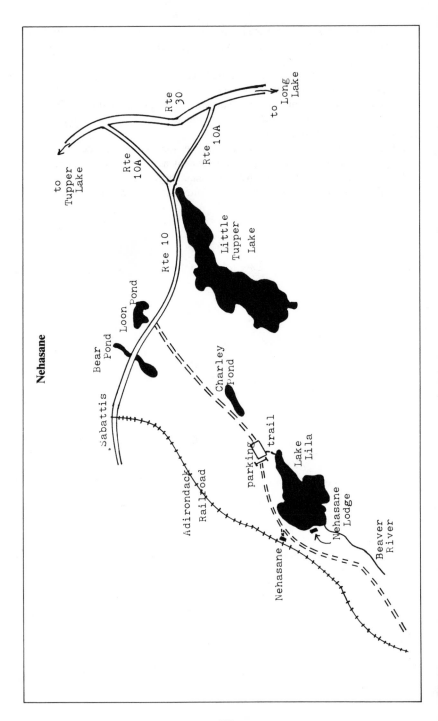

Nehasane

12. Nehasane

Nehasane (Ne-haas'in-nee) is treated here as a separate section, but it is anticipated that at least some of this land will eventually become part of the Five Ponds Wilderness Area.

One of the earliest settlers of this part of the Adirondacks was David Smith, a hermit at Smith Lake from 1830–1845. The lake has since been called Lake Lila, after the wife of Dr. Seward Webb. This lake is the largest lake in the Forest Preserve whose perimeter is entirely owned by New York State.

While president of the Wagner Palace Car Company, the manufacturer of Pullman Railroad Cars, Webb started the Adirondack and St. Lawrence Railroad. This was consolidated with the Mohawk and Malone (M & M) Railroad Company, which had a private stop at Nehasane. This same track operates today as the Adirondack Railroad. It runs from Utica to Lake Placid (1980). This allows the hiker to take the train right to Nehasane, where hiking begins the moment you step off the train.

The Nehasane Park Association was created in 1894. The great Nehasane Lodge once housed twenty-five guests and servants. Now unoccupied, it is scheduled to be demolished (1980). Webb introduced black-tailed deer and elk to his fenced-in preserve. Gifford Pinchot, the famous early forest management expert, wrote his book *The Adirondack Spruce* while employed at Nehasane. It was the first American publication to explain how European forest management systems could be applied in the United States.

Nehasane

Difficulty: Easy canoeing, hard backpacking.
Time Needed: Variable
Maps: Big Moose 15′ Series and
    Five Ponds 15′ Series

Access to Nehasane is off Rte. 30 between Long Lake and Tupper Lake. Whichever direction you are coming from, turn west on either of the two roads (0.0 mi.) having signs indicating the direction to Sabattis. They merge after 3.1 mi. (5.0 km) at Little Tupper Lake, continuing as County Road 10 down the north side of the lake for Sabattis. The headquarters for Whitney Park is passed at 4.4 mi. (7.1 km). Be careful not to miss the turn-off for Nehasane Park as you come down a dip in the road at 8.3 mi. (13.4 km). Turn left onto the dirt road and proceed another 5.9 mi. (9.6 km). At that point a DEC parking area is reached near Lake Lila. A gate at the opposite end of the parking area prevents further vehicular traffic. No trailers for camping or boats are permitted here. No hunting on surrounding private lands is permitted, whether or not the land has been posted.

Recreational opportunities at Nehasane have not yet been fully developed (1980). It will be several years before land classifications have been designated and proper unit management plans reflect the best use for this land. Several options are nonetheless available to the camper.

Maps of Lake Lila are available at the DEC trail register in the parking area, and a Park Ranger is on duty in the general area. A trail from the parking area leads 0.3 mi. (0.5 km) down a slight grade to the sandy beach on Lake Lila. Here canoes and other nonmotorized watercraft can be put into the water. Only cartop-carried craft are allowed.

Camping is permitted at fourteen areas around the shoreline and on four islands. Each site is marked by orange tape or signs, and each has a limited size. Camping is also permitted at other points around the lake, but the camper must be at least 150 ft. (46 m) back from the shore. No camping is allowed in or near any buildings.

At the present time, recreational opportunities are best for the canoer. Day trips inland are possible, however. From the parking area gate, the hiker can walk along the dirt road 1.5 mi. (2.4 km) to the lake shore. Still further along this road, at 3.2 mi. (5.2 km), the site of Nehasane Lodge is reached.

Pratt's Mountain (sometimes called Smith's Summit or Summit Rock) rises 500 ft. (153 m) above Lake Lila. Mount Fredricks is inland a bit, but also is frequently climbed. Still further inland is a trail up Mount Electra.

The experienced woodsman or backwoods skier can travel to Niger Lake (Negro Lake on older maps) by swinging northwest, where Forest Preserve land leads into the Five Ponds Wilderness Area. Pigeon Lake Wilderness Area is to the west. The expert backpacker can bushwhack through this country, but it is definitely not advised for the novice since there are few, if any, trails here. Because a lot of the land is privately owned and the trails indicated on the dated maps are undependable, anyone contemplating going into this region should plan his trip very carefully.

INDEX

115

Vermont 23, 34, 37
Vittles 16
Vly, The 38

Wagner Palace Car Co. 111
Wakely Dam 55–57
Wallface Mt. 93–94, 96
Wallface Ponds 94–96
Wanakena 101–102, 105
Ward Pond 85
Warren County 49
Washbowl 107
Wells 45
West Canada Creek 53
West Canada Lakes 53, 55–57, 60
West Canada Mt. 53
West Lake 53, 56
West Mt. 76–77, 80, 82–83
West Stony Creek 48
Wevertown 45
Whale Tail Mt. 95
Whitehall 29, 31
Whitney Park 111

Whortleberry Pond 18
Wilcox Lake 45–46, 48–49
Wilcox Mt. 49
Wild Forests 5
Wilderness 5
Willis Mt. 49
Winona Lake 45
Winter Camping 1
Winter Green Point 27
Wolf Creek 55
Wolf Lake 53, 55–56
Wolf Landing 64
Wolf Mt. 101
Wolf Pond 25–26, 102, 105, 107
Wolf Pond Mt. 85
Woodhull Creek 62, 67–68
Woodhull Lake (Big) 62–64, 66–68
Woodhull Mt. 62, 64
Woodgate 62, 65–66
Wright Peak 95

Yellowstone National Park 5
Yosemite National Park 5

INDEX OF PEOPLE

Batcheller, Irving 104
Belden Brothers 53
Brown, Grace 77
Brownell 49
Byron-Curtis, Rev. A. L. 63

Campbell, Duncan 29
Carter, Cornelius 105
Conkling, Bert 63
Conkling, Roscoe 63

Dean, Joan 108
Dewey, Melville 93
Dreiser, Theodore 77
Dutton, William 77

Emmons, Ebenezer 96

Fielding, Matilda 99
Fielding, Mr. 99
Foster, Nat 63
French Louie 53

Gillette, Chester 77
Griffin 102

Haskell, Traume 53
Hicks 100
Higby, James 77
Henderson, David 93, 97
Howell, Lucretia 53

Jogues, Father Isaac 29

Knox, Henry 29

Leary, Arthur 105

McGuire, Phil 63
McMartin 98
Montcalm, Marquis de 29
Munro, Colonel 29

Nye, William 99

Parker, Captain 88
Piche 91
Pinchot, Gifford 109

Roger's Rangers 29

Sabattis, Mitchell 88
Scott, Philo (Fide) 104
Sheppard, Jack 77
Smith, David 111
Strong, Silas 104

Van Hoevenberg 99

Wakely, William 39
Webb, Dr. William Seward 101, 111
West 98
Wright, Jonathan (Jock) 63

ABOUT THE AUTHOR

Bruce Wadsworth is a science educator in Delmar, New York. He holds a B.A. from Alfred University, an M.S. from Syracuse University, and a post-graduate degree in Administration and Supervision from SUNY at Albany. He has attended National Science Foundation Institutes in Geology of North America at Vassar, and in Cytology and Biochemistry at Alfred University. In 1971 he studied Adirondack biosystems at the Cranberry Lake Biological Station, SUNY School of Forestry and Environmental Sciences at Syracuse.

His family of four became "46 'ers" in 1976 after climbing each of the High Peaks together, and he has been an "end-to-ender" on the Northville-Placid Trail twice. Early spring usually finds him clearing trails in the Silver Lake Wilderness Area. Special interests include wilderness preservation and Adirondack history. He is an active member of the Adirondack Mountain Club.

Other Publications
of
The Adirondack Mountain Club, Inc.
174 Glen Street
Glens Falls, N.Y. 12801
(518) 793-7737

Guidebooks

GUIDE TO ADIRONDACK TRAILS: HIGH PEAKS REGION. *Eleventh edition.* Includes separate topo map. Definitive guide to the High Peaks.

GUIDE TO THE NORTHVILLE—PLACID TRAIL. Detailed description and guide to 133-mile trail; contains page maps for each section and separate topo map.

GUIDE TO TRAILS OF THE WEST-CENTRAL ADIRONDACKS. Hiking trails and canoe route from Old Forge area to Blue Mountain Lake.

GUIDE TO ADIRONDACK TRAILS: NORTHERN REGION

GUIDE TO ADIRONDACK TRAILS: CENTRAL REGION

GUIDE TO THE EASTERN ADIRONDACKS. Trails, paths, bushwhacks in the lake George Region, the Pharaoh Lake Wilderness Area, and beyond.

ADIRONDACK CANOE WATERS—NORTH FLOW. *Second edition.* Definitive guide to 700 miles of canoe routes in St. Lawrence/Lake Champlain drainage basins.

ADIRONDACK CANOE WATERS—SOUTH AND WEST FLOW. Guide to canoe waters of the Black River Basin, the Mohawk Basin, the Upper Hudson Basin and the two major streams of the Tug Hill Plateau.

AN ADIRONDACK SAMPLER, Day Hikes for All Seasons. A sampling of hikes throughout the Park for the single-day forest traveler.

Natural History

TREES OF THE ADIRONDACK HIGH PEAK REGION. Hiker's identification guide to trees in the Forest Preserve.

THE ADIRONDACK LANDSCAPE. Complete hiker's guide to common High Peak landforms.

ROCK SCENERY OF THE HUDSON HIGHLANDS AND PALISADES. Guide to the geology of southern New York State.

How-to

WINTER HIKING AND CAMPING. Authoritative basic manual on winter wilderness excursions.

General Reading

PEAKS AND PEOPLE OF THE ADIRONDACKS. Geography and lore of the Adirondack High Peaks.

TALES FROM THE SHAWANGUNK MOUNTAINS. A naturalist's musings, a bushwhacker's guide.

ADIRONDACK READER. An anthology of the best writings about the region.

ADIRONDACK PILGRIMAGE. A collection of essays and reviews by Paul Jamieson.

Maps

Trails of the Adirondack High Peaks Region
USGS quads of Marcy, Santanoni, half of Elizabethtown; Wilmington, Lake Placid, half of Lewis, half of Saranac Lake

Trails of the West-Central Adirondacks
Old Forge area to Blue Mountain Lake

Trails of the Central Region
USGS quads of Schroon Lake, Blue Mt., Indian Lake, Newcomb, Thirteenth Lake

Trails of the Northern Region
USGS quads of Fine, Oswegatchie, Oswegatchie SW, Oswegatchie SE, Newton Falls, Cranberry Lake, Wolf Mt., Five Ponds

Trails of the Eastern Region

Price List available on request